W9-CAU-755

Can God Be Free?

Can God Be Free?

William L. Rowe

CLARENDON PRESS · OXFORD

OXFORD
UNIVERSITY PRESS

Great Clarendon Street, Oxford OX2 6DP

Oxford University Press is a department of the University of Oxford.
It furthers the University's objective of excellence in research, scholarship,
and education by publishing worldwide in

Oxford New York

Auckland Bangkok Buenos Aires Cape Town Chennai
Dar es Salaam Delhi Hong Kong Istanbul Karachi Kolkata
Kuala Lumpur Madrid Melbourne Mexico City Mumbai Nairobi
São Paulo Shanghai Taipei Tokyo Toronto

Oxford is a registered trade mark of Oxford University Press
in the UK and in certain other countries

Published in the United States
by Oxford University Press Inc., New York.

British Library Cataloguing in Publication Data

Data available

Library of Congress Cataloging in Publication Data

Data available

ISBN 0-19-825045-2

1 3 5 7 9 10 8 6 4 2

Typeset by 10.25 on 12.5pt DanteMT
Kolam Information Services Pvt. Ltd, Pondicherry, India
Printed in Great Britain
on acid-free paper by
Biddles Ltd., King's Lynn, Norfolk

For Ellen and Lucas Rowe

Acknowledgments

This book has been a long time in the making. I began thinking about the problem of Divine Perfection and Freedom after reading Wes Morriston's important paper, 'Is God Significantly Free?', published in 1985. The guiding idea for the book appeared in print as early as 1993 with the publication of my paper entitled 'The Problem of Divine Perfection and Freedom'. In 1998, after a discussion with Oxford's editor Peter Momtchiloff at the December meeting of the American Philosophical Association, I developed a proposal for Oxford University Press for a book to be entitled 'Can God Be Free?' Along the way various commitments prevented me from completing the manuscript in a timely fashion, and I am grateful to Peter both for his patience and continuing support of this project.

Colleagues both at Purdue and elsewhere have been exceedingly generous with their time in discussing with me some of the central ideas and arguments that appear in this book. Among those in the profession to whom I am particularly grateful for help, advice, and criticisms are Marilyn Adams, Robert Adams, William Alston, Michael Bergmann, Jeff Brower, Jan Cover, Paul Draper, John Martin Fischer, William Hasker, Dan Howard-Snyder, Frances Howard-Snyder, Jeff Jordan, Norman Kretzmann, Bruce Langtry, Scott MacDonald, George Mavrodes, Thomas V. Morris, Wes Morriston, Phil Quinn, Eleonore Stump, William Wainwright, David Widerker, Edward Wierenga, and Stephen Wykstra.

Students, too, have helped me. In the Fall of 2002 I taught a graduate level course at Purdue University on the topic of divine and human freedom. Over half of the course concerned the problem of divine freedom. For this part of the course students were asked to read sections of the manuscript of this book, along with written criticisms provided by the Howard-Snyders, Bill Hasker, Edward Wierenga, and William Wainwright. A number of these students made quite helpful contributions both in discussion and in written papers. I am indebted to them for their keen interest in the topics considered in the course, their helpful discussion of these topics, as well as their criticisms of some of the central arguments I advance in this book. The students who took the course are Bertha Alvarez, Tully Borland, Andrew Brei, Gregory Daly, Nathan Dickman, Justin Ho, Joel Krueger, Christopher Manon, Justin Marquis, Jack Mulder, Daniel Newhart, Krista Paradiso, Myron Penner, Thad Robinson, Ron Rowe, Kevin Sharpe, Brad Sickler, and Winship Varner.

Parts of chapters in this book were presented in the following places: a Department of Philosophy Colloquium, Syracuse University, December, 1992; the Philosophy of Religion Society meeting in conjunction with the Pacific Division Meeting of the APA, San Francisco, March, 1993; the Rocky Mountain Society for Christian Philosophers Meeting, University of Colorado, April 1997; Bar Ilan University, Israel, March, 1998; the University of West Virginia, October 1999; and the Society for Philosophy of Religion, Hilton Head Island, February, 2001.

To the Center for Humanistic Studies of The School of Liberal arts at Purdue University I am indebted for a fellowship enabling me to work full-time on this topic during the Spring term of 1996.

W. L. R.

Contents

Introduction

When religion was in its infancy, it was natural for human beings to envisage the gods as both different from us, and somewhat like us—having greater longevity, as well as greater power, residing in the heavens rather than on earth, but still somewhat limited in power and knowledge, jealous of other gods, and sometimes at war with one another. But as the great religions slowly developed, there emerged the idea of a single god, a being of great wisdom, power, and goodness. In the West, this majestic idea of God was developed and refined over the centuries by influential theologians such as Augustine, Boethius, Bonaventure, Avicenna, Anselm, Maimonides, and Aquinas. It is now the dominant conception of God in the three great religions of the West: Judaism, Christianity, and Islam. God is no longer thought of as just a great being, or even the greatest being among all beings that have ever existed or ever will exist. God is thought of as *the greatest possible being*, the being than which none greater exists or can even be conceived to exist. Quite naturally, then, God is taken to be a being whose goodness, knowledge, and power is such that it is inconceivable and logically impossible for any being, including God himself, to have a greater degree of goodness, knowledge, and power. Moreover, as part of his essential greatness, God is thought to be a necessarily existing being, a being who exists and logically could not fail to exist.

Slowly, over the centuries since the emergence of this idea of God, conceptual difficulties have been raised concerning it. A very simple one concerns God's infinite power. It asks whether God is so powerful that he can make a stone so heavy he can't lift it. If he can make such a stone, then there is something he cannot do—lift the stone that he can make. If he can't make such a stone, then there is also something he is unable to do—create such a stone. Most philosophers believe that this problem is a shallow one and can be solved without much difficulty, although there remains disagreement concerning which way of solving it is the best. Perhaps the simplest way around it is to say that God cannot create such a stone, for it is impossible for there to exist a stone so heavy that God cannot lift it or otherwise cause it to rise from where it rests. And most religious thinkers hold, with Thomas Aquinas, that power extends only to what is logically possible to be done. Since, by virtue of God's possessing *maximal* power, it is impossible for there to be an object so heavy that God can't lift it, for God to make such a stone is for God's power to extend to bringing something into existence that logically cannot exist. And since power, no matter how great, extends only to what is logically possible for God to do, the fact that God cannot create an impossible stone fails to show any limitation on God's power.

The issue that serves as the center of this book focuses not on problems concerning God's power, but problems concerning his *freedom* and *praiseworthiness* in relation to his *perfect goodness*. Given his necessary perfections, if there is a best world for God to create then it appears he would have no choice other than to create it. For, as Leibniz tells us, 'to do less good than one could is to be lacking in wisdom or in goodness'. Since it is strictly impossible for God to be lacking in wisdom or goodness, his inability to do otherwise than create the best possible world is no limitation on his power. But if God could not do otherwise than create the best world, he created the world of necessity, and not freely. And, if that is so, it may be argued that we have no reason to be thankful to God for creating us, since, being parts of the best possible world, God was simply unable to do anything other than create us—he created us of necessity, not freely. Moreover, we are confronted with the further difficulty of having to believe that this world, with its holocaust, and innumerable other evils, is the best that an infinitely powerful, infinitely good being could do in creating a world. Neither of these conclusions, taken by itself, seems at all plausible. Yet each conclusion appears to follow from the conception of God now dominant in the great religions of the West. In this book I undertake the study of this problem, both historically in the writings of Gottfried Leibniz, Samuel Clarke, Thomas Aquinas, and Jonathan Edwards, as well as in the contemporary philosophical literature devoted to this important problem. I believe the problem is more serious than is commonly thought and may require some significant revision in contemporary thinking about the nature of God.

Leibniz (1646–1716) envisaged God as selecting from a vast array of possible worlds the one he then wills to create. But which one does he select? For reasons we will consider in Chapter 1, Leibniz held that there

must be a single world that is the best among all the possible worlds. ↗
he reasoned that God's perfect goodness requires him to create tl
world. But if that is so, can it also be true that God's decision with respe..
to creation was a *free* decision? For, since being perfectly good is part of
God's very nature, it is impossible for God to have done otherwise than
create the best world. And if God couldn't have done other than create
the best world, either he is not free at all with respect to creation or his
freedom is of a different sort altogether from the freedom to do good or
bad that we ascribe to ourselves. My own view, as developed in the
chapters that follow, is that this particular problem of perfection and
freedom can be solved only by ascribing to God a different sort of
freedom. That is, a freedom to do what is good that does not include
the freedom to do what is bad or the freedom to do less good than one
can. Within the theistic tradition there are resources for such a solution.
For example, in the *City of God* Augustine (354–430) suggests that God is
free by virtue of having the power always to choose and act in accordance with his knowledge of what is best. And he points out that while the
freedom the creature has includes the ability to do what is bad, God *by
nature* cannot do what is bad. (Another major theologian and philosopher who ascribes to God a sort of freedom that precludes the power to
choose less than the best is Anselm (1033–1109)). While this different
sort of freedom finds some support in the history of Western religious
thought, it is opposed by those who insist that God must be able *to do
otherwise* if he is to enjoy any kind of significant freedom. Moreover, the
Augustinian solution faces the serious problem of providing grounds for
our being *grateful* to God for doing what is best. For gratitude to
someone for what that person does seems to presuppose a belief that
the person could have refrained from doing that thing. But on Augustine's view of God such belief appears to be unwarranted. God's nature
necessarily precludes his refraining from doing what he sees to be the
best course of action.

Leibniz thought that the existence of God was sufficiently established
to enable us to draw some conclusions about the actual world in which
we exist. First, he concluded, of course, that the actual world was created
by God. Second, he concluded that the actual world is the best of all
possible worlds. Although this conclusion was satirized by Voltaire, and
may seem doubtful to anyone who reflects on the enormous amount of
evil in our world, Leibniz mounted strong arguments for the conclusion
that this world is the best possible world. He reasoned that God's

perfections would require him to create the best world he could, that being all-powerful God could create any world he chose to create, and that God could have a sufficient reason to create a world only if among possible worlds there is one that is better than all others. From these assumptions it does follow that if God exists, the actual world is the best of all possible worlds. In the first chapter we will look with some care at Leibniz's reasoning and consider at length a central objection to it: that it cannot avoid the conclusion that God is not sufficiently free in creating, and is therefore not a fit subject of gratitude or moral praise for creating the best. We will also consider (Chapter 2) the view of a prominent contemporary of Leibniz, the English philosopher and theologian Samuel Clarke (1675–1729). Clarke and Leibniz both hold that the world God creates is the best possible world. But, unlike Leibniz, Clarke holds that God is free in the sense of having the power not to create the best. We will consider whether Clarke's position on this matter can be reasonably defended and explore the various alternatives that may be held with respect to God's freedom given that among worlds there is a best world.

A very important, historical alternative to the Leibniz–Clarke view holds that among worlds God considers for creation there simply is no best world. The idea here is not that there are a number of worlds equally good and none better, but that for any world, however great its degree of goodness, there is a possible world better than it. This view is found in Aquinas (1225–74) and other religious thinkers. What are we to say about the world God creates, if this view is correct? For on the assumption that for every creatable world there is a better creatable world, it is logically impossible for God to create the best world. The prevailing and initially plausible view is that it would not be inconsistent with God's perfect goodness for him to create a very good world, even though he could have created a better world. For creating no world at all hardly seems preferable to creating a very good world, even if there is a better world than it that God could have created instead. But against this view there is a serious argument to the effect that no such being as God could even exist if for every creatable world there is a better creatable world. This argument depends on the following principle:

> If an omniscient being creates a world when it could have created a better world then it is possible that there be a being morally better than it.

From this principle and the assumption that for any creatable world there is a better creatable world, it follows that an all-powerful, omniscient creator of a world is a being than which a better being is possible. But the theistic God is by nature an unsurpassable being, a being than which a better being is not possible. Therefore, so the argument goes, if there is no best world, the exalted God of Judaism, Christianity, and Islam does not exist.

The 'principle' cited above, is, as one might expect, enormously controversial. Indeed, very significant objections have been raised against it. One formidable objection goes as follows. First, it is argued that there is a strong analogy between God's power and his goodness. Second, it is noted that failure to bring about what is logically impossible is no limitation on God's power. Third, it is observed that if for every creatable world there is a better creatable world, then it is logically impossible for God to create the best world he can. Therefore, so the argument goes, the fact that God cannot create the best world he can implies no limitation on his power. Finally, the analogy between God's power and his goodness suggests that failure to do the best that he can in creating a world (when doing the best he can is logically impossible) is no limitation on God's perfect goodness. So, the objection concludes, the principle cited above is false. The fact that for any world he creates God could have created a better world does not imply that God could have been better than he is.

A related objection that has been advanced against the principle cited above suggests that the principle is applicable only when it is possible for a being to do the best it can. If there is no best world then it is not possible for God to do the best he can. If there is a best among creatable worlds, then it is possible for God to do the best that he can. For he can do this by creating the best world. If a being *could* create the best world but does not, then, so the suggestion goes, the principle may be applicable, resulting in the conclusion that the being in question is not unsurpassable. But when it is impossible for a being to do the best it can—as is the case for an all-powerful, all-knowing being when for every creatable world there is a better creatable world—then it seems wrong to insist on the principle. For to insist on its applicability in the no best world scenario is just to beg the question concerning the existence of God.

These are important objections. They, and others, will be carefully considered in the chapters of this book. We shall begin, however, with the Leibnizian view that God is free with respect to creation, that God's perfection requires him to create the best possible world, and that this world, therefore, is the best possible world. As we shall see, Leibniz's view of freedom is a version of *compatibilism*, the view that a decision or action may be freely performed even though it is determined to occur by earlier events or facts over which the agent may have no control. Another idea of freedom, *libertarianism*, maintains that an agent's decision or action is freely performed only if at the time of the decision it was in the agent's power then and there to refrain from bringing about that decision. On the libertarian view it is strictly impossible that an agent's decision be a free decision if it was determined to occur by earlier events over which the agent had no control. Samuel Clarke upheld the libertarian view of freedom in opposition to Leibniz's compatibilism with respect to freedom. Since how we conceive of *freedom*, including divine freedom, is critical to answering our main question, Can God be Free?, we can do no better than begin our study with a discussion of the famous exchange between Leibniz (the compatibilist) and Clarke (the libertarian). Upon completing our study of Leibniz (Chapter 1) and Clarke (Chapter 2), we will examine Aquinas's discussion of divine freedom in relation to his view that there is no best possible world (Chapter 3). This will provide us an opportunity to examine the view, held by Aquinas, both that there is an infinity of increasingly better creatable worlds and that God enjoys freedom in selecting the world he will create. Our study of Aquinas's view will be followed by an examination of the position on divine (and human) freedom advocated by the important American theologian and philosopher, Jonathan Edwards (1704–58). Unlike Aquinas, Edwards develops an explicitly *compatibilist* account of freedom, both divine and human, and insists, with Leibniz, that our world is the best of all possible worlds.

After examining these four historically important views of divine and human freedom, in Chapters 5–7 we will consider some of the contemporary literature concerning divine freedom with respect to creation. In Chapter 5 we examine an influential essay by Robert Adams in which he argues on moral grounds that even if there is a best world, God would be free to create some good world less than the best. And in the longest chapter in the book, Chapter 6, we continue the study of the large body of important, contemporary literature defending the view that God is perfectly free to create a world even when there is a better world he can create instead. Along the way we will also consider the possibility that although there is no best world there are a number of worlds equally good and none better—a view that appears to leave God free to select from among those equally good worlds the one he will create. As I've indicated, the overall conclusion of this book—tentative as it may be—is that God cannot enjoy much in the way of libertarian freedom with respect to creation. This conclusion is opposed to the conclusion reached in the large body of literature examined in Chapter 6. In addition I argue that other non-libertarian notions of freedom in which God may be said to be free with respect to creation are insufficient to support our being thankful and grateful to God for creating the world he has created. As noted in Chapter 7, however, the conclusions reached are based on the supposition that God is not responsible for his having the absolute perfections that are part of his nature—for he played no causal role in his having those perfections. So, in that chapter we consider whether or not God can be the cause of his own nature, and thus may be causally responsible for the perfect nature that constrains his freedom.

While the conclusions reached in this book may be more tentative than we would like, or not the conclusions that are theologically satisfying, grappling with these issues will deepen our understanding of classical theism and of one of the philosophical issues in theism that has fascinated philosophers and theologians for centuries.

1

Leibniz on Divine Perfection and Freedom[1]

In 1715 a series of written exchanges began between the eminent, highly original German philosopher Gottfried Leibniz and the brilliant British theologian Samuel Clarke. Halted by Leibniz's death in 1716, the series was edited and published by Clarke in 1717.[2] The occasion for the exchange was Leibniz's remark in a letter to Caroline, Princess of Wales, that Newtonian physics had contributed to the decline of natural religion in England.[3] Since Clarke, a learned theologian and philosopher, was both closely associated with Newton and had been personally acquainted with the Stuart royalty through serving as chaplain to Queen Anne, he took up the defense of both natural religion in England and Newtonian views of absolute space and time. In the process of their discussions a deep divergence emerged in their respective views of freedom, both human and divine. From these exchanges, as well as their other writings, much can be learned about the philosophical similarities and differences between these two great exponents of theo-

---

[1] A substantial portion of the material on Leibniz (Chapter 1) and Clarke (Chapter 2) is taken (with permission) from my essay 'Clarke and Leibniz on Divine Perfection and Freedom', *Enlightenment and Dissent* (Special Issue on Samuel Clarke, ed. James Dybikowski), 16 (1997), 60–82.

[2] Samuel Clarke and Gottfried Leibniz, *The Leibniz–Clarke Correspondence* (1717), ed. H. G. Alexander (Manchester: Manchester University Press, 1956). References to the Leibniz–Clarke Correspondence will be incorporated in the text as LC, followed by the appropriate page number in Alexander's edition.

[3] An earlier controversy over the discovery of the calculus had caused some bitterness between Newton and Leibniz. So, Leibniz's remark to Princess Caroline was not likely to be ignored by Newton's friends and supporters.

logical rationalism.[4] Clarke and Leibniz agreed that human reason can demonstrate that there necessarily exists an essentially omnipotent, omniscient, perfectly good being who has freely created the world.[5] But, as I've indicated, their accounts of divine freedom were profoundly different. My concern here is to highlight their differences over divine freedom and to consider whether either conception of divine freedom can be reconciled with the absolute perfection of the creator. In this chapter we will look at some of the fundamental differences between Leibniz and Clarke, and carefully examine Leibniz's view of divine freedom. In the next chapter we will consider Clarke's radically different view of freedom, both human and divine. I will argue that neither conception can be fully reconciled with the requirement imposed by God's perfect goodness; in Clarke's words, 'the necessity of always doing what is best'.

In addition to Leibniz's attacks on Newton's natural philosophy and Clarke's replies on behalf of Newton, an important issue in the Leibniz–Clarke correspondence concerns the Principle of Sufficient Reason (PSR), particularly its implications for how we must understand divine and human freedom. In his second letter Leibniz advances the principle and pronounces on its implications for theology and metaphysics. 'Now, by that single principle, viz. that there ought to be a sufficient reason why things should be so, and not otherwise, one may demonstrate the being of a God, and all the other parts of metaphysics or natural theology' (LC, 16).[6] He illustrates PSR by citing the example of Archimedes who observed that if there be a perfect balance, and if

---

[4] By 'theological rationalism' I mean the view that unaided human reason is capable of demonstrating the necessary existence and nature of God, as God is traditionally conceived within the major theistic religions of the West.

[5] Leibniz made use of both the ontological argument and the cosmological argument. Clarke had doubts about the ontological argument. But he developed a strong version of the cosmological argument for this purpose. See *A Demonstration of the Being and Attributes of God* (1705; 9th edn., London: printed by W. Botham for John and Paul Knapton, 1738). Further references to this work will be incorporated in the text as D, followed by the appropriate page number. References to works by Clarke other than this work and his correspondence with Leibniz will be to the appropriate volume and page numbers of the reprinting of his *Works* (1738) in four volumes in *British Philosophers and Theologians of the 17th and 18th Centuries* (New York: Garland, 1978). Quotations from Clarke's works, other than his correspondence with Leibniz, have been modernized in terms of punctuation, spelling, and use of capitals.

[6] Leibniz elsewhere expresses PSR more fully as the principle '... that no fact can be real or existent, no statement true, unless there be a sufficient reason why it is so and not otherwise, ...': Gottfried Leibniz, *Monadology* (1714), para. 32, in *Leibniz Selections*, ed. Philip P. Wiener (New York: Charles Scribner's Sons, 1951).

equal weights are hung on the two ends of that balance, the balance will not move. Why? Leibniz answers: 'It is because no reason can be given, why one side should weigh down, rather than another' (LC, 16). It was perhaps unfortunate for Leibniz to use this example.[7] For it enabled Clarke to charge him with treating an agent no differently from a balance: just as the balance cannot move without a greater weight on one side, and must move downward on the side with the greater weight, so the agent cannot choose without some motive to choose, and must choose in accordance with the strongest motive. But, Clarke argues, this is to deny the agent any power to act in the absence of a motive, and to deny the agent any power to act in opposition to the strongest motive. It is, in Clarke's view, to deny that there are any genuine agents at all. For it is the nature of an agent to have the power to act or not act. A balance has no such power; it is simply acted upon by whatever weights are placed upon it. As Clarke concludes in his fifth and final reply:

There is no similitude between a balance being moved by weights or impulse, and a mind moving itself, or acting upon the view of certain motives. The difference is, that the one is entirely passive; which is being subject to absolute necessity: the other not only is acted upon, but acts also; which is the essence of liberty. (LC, 97)

Clarke's rejection of any 'similitude' between the movements of a balance and the acts of an agent is closely connected to his disagreement with Leibniz over PSR. In his response to the second letter Clarke *appears* to accept PSR. Thus he says: 'It is very true, that nothing is, without a sufficient reason why it is, and why it is thus rather than otherwise' (LC, 20). Clearly, if when writing 'nothing is' Clarke means to include any fact or truth whatever, then he cannot consistently go on, as he does, to exempt certain facts or truths from the necessity of having a sufficient reason. Leibniz may have read Clarke's 'nothing is' as encompassing any fact or truth whatever, which would approach Leibniz's own understanding of PSR. If so, this would explain why in his third letter he complains that although Clarke grants him this important principle, 'he grants it only in words, and in reality denies it. Which shows that he does not fully perceive the strength of it' (LC, 25). However, despite his

---

[7] Leibniz draws the example from Bayle. See Leibniz's *Theodicy*, trans. E. M. Huggard, ed. Austin Farrer (LaSalle, Ill.: Open Court 1985), 321–2. Further references to this work will be incorporated in the text as T, followed by the appropriate page number.

statement 'nothing is, without a sufficient reason why it is,' it is clear that Clarke cannot have intended to agree with Leibniz that *every* fact or truth has a sufficient reason. Nor could he have agreed that *every contingent* fact or truth has a sufficient reason. For he immediately goes on to say that 'this sufficient reason is oft-times no other, than the mere will of God,' citing as an example God's volition to create this system of matter in one particular place within absolute space, rather than in some other place in absolute space. There is simply nothing to recommend one particular place in absolute space over another. Hence, in this case there can be no other reason than the mere will of God.[8] In his third letter Leibniz cites this case as just the sort of thing that PSR rules out as impossible. On his understanding of PSR there can be no situations at all in which a choice has been made without a sufficient reason for making *that particular choice*.[9] To think otherwise is to suppose an exception to PSR. It is clear that Clarke allows for such exceptions.

A deeper and more important disagreement concerning PSR is also reflected in Clarke's reaction to Leibniz's analogy between the sufficient reason for the balance to move and the sufficient reason for an agent to do one thing rather than another. For Clarke agrees with Leibniz that often enough the agent has a sufficient reason for her action. So, he allows that PSR is satisfied for a vast array of human and divine acts. What he denies is that the sufficient reason for the agent doing one thing rather than another operates on the agent in the way in which the heavier weight operates on the balance. Clearly, the heavier weight on one side of the balance is a *determining cause* of the movement of the balance. Given the circumstances and the placement of that weight on the one side of the balance, nothing else could happen than what did happen, it was *necessary* that the balance move as it did. But to suppose that the reason or motive that is the sufficient reason for the agent to do one thing rather than another is a *determining cause* of the agent's act is to deny any power on the agent's part to perform or not perform that particular act. It is to render the agent's act *necessary* and to deny the

[8] Presumably, Clarke would say that God had a sufficient reason to create this system of matter in *some place or other* in absolute space, but he did not have a sufficient reason to create it in this *particular place*.

[9] Leibniz does allow that there are many human acts that *appear* to lack a sufficient reason. There are acts for which we cannot find a sufficient motive. For example, no motive is apparent for why an agent stepped over the threshold with his left foot rather than his right. But Leibniz supposed that in all such cases there is some unconscious perception or passion that provides the sufficient reason.

agent's freedom of will. Thus, for Clarke, a reason or motive may be the sufficient reason for the agent's action. But, unlike the weight in the balance that is the determining cause of the movement of the balance, the reason or motive is not the determining cause of the agent's act. As he puts it elsewhere:

Occasions indeed they (reasons and motives) may be, and are, upon which that substance in man, wherein the self-moving principle resides, freely exerts its active power. But it is the self-moving principle, and not at all the reason or motive, which is the physical or efficient cause of action. When we say, in vulgar speech, that motives or reason *determine* a man; it is not but a figure or metaphor. It is the man that freely determines himself to act.[10]

What we've seen is that Clarke's conception of what it is to be a free agent requires first that the agent may act in some *particular way* even in the absence of his having a sufficient reason to act in that particular way. Thus, there are exceptions to PSR. Second, we've seen that when the agent has a sufficient reason to do a particular act and *freely* does that act, the sufficient reason or motive is not a *determining cause* of the agent's act. At the time of the act the agent had the power not to perform that act. So, on Clarke's view there is a profound difference between the sufficient reason for the balance moving in a particular way and the sufficient reason for an agent's free act. In the first case the sufficient reason is a determining cause, in the second it is not. Leibniz, however, sees no need to suppose there are exceptions to PSR and no need to treat the motive for the agent's free act as anything other than a *determining cause* of that act.

With this background in place, we can now look at the problem of divine perfection and freedom and then consider the very different solutions proposed by Leibniz and Clarke to that problem. Following Leibniz, we can imagine God considering a variety of worlds he might create. One might be a world in which there are no conscious creatures at all, a world composed solely of dead matter.[11] Another might be a world composed (at some stage in its history) of living, conscious creatures whose lives are meaningful, morally good, and happy. If we imagine God making a choice between these two worlds, it seems evident that he would create the latter. Surely, a world with conscious

---

[10] *Works* (Garland, edn.), iv. 723.

[11] Of course, given that the actual world includes everything that exists, including God, the world in question is here being considered *apart from God*.

creatures living morally good, satisfying lives is, other things being equal, a very good world, and *better than* a world consisting of nothing but dull bits of matter swirling endlessly in a void. And isn't it absolutely certain that an omnipotent, omniscient, perfectly good being would create the *better* world if he could? But if we pursue this line of thought, problems begin to emerge. Assume, as seems evident, that the second world is the better world. If God were limited to these two worlds, he would face three choices: creating the inferior world, creating the superior world, creating no world at all. For God to decide to create no world over creating a world that is, all things considered, a very good world, would be for God to do less than the best that he can do.[12] If so, it seems that God's perfect goodness would *require* him to create the very good world. But if God's perfect goodness requires him to create the very good world, rather than creating the inferior world or not creating a world at all, what are we to make of that part of the idea of God that declares that he created the world *freely*? To say that God *freely* created the good world seems to imply that he was free not to do so, that he could have created the inferior world, or refrained from creating either world. But if his perfect goodness *requires* him to create the good world, how is it possible that he was free to create the inferior world or not to create any world? This is a simple way of picturing the problem of divine perfection and divine freedom.

Initially, one may be tempted to solve this problem by viewing God's perfect goodness (which includes his absolute moral perfection) as analogous to our goodness. A morally good person may actually do the very best action available to her while being free not to do it, or free to do something bad instead. Of course, had she freely done the bad thing, she would have exhibited some sort of moral failing. But the mere fact that she was *free* to have done the bad thing doesn't impugn whatever degree of moral goodness she possesses. So why should God's perfect goodness preclude his being free to create a less good world, or even a bad world? Had he done that, he would have ceased being the morally perfect being he is, just as the morally good person would have diminished somewhat her moral goodness had she freely done the wrong thing.

---

[12] We will later see the importance of distinguishing between God's *not deciding* to create a world and God's *deciding not* to create a world.

This solution fails because, although a human person *can* become less good or even bad, God *cannot* become less than absolutely perfect. Although we may achieve a certain degree of moral virtue in our lives, we can lose it and sink back into being the morally mediocre persons we perhaps once were. This is because it is not part of our very nature to be at a certain level of goodness. According to the historically dominant view in Western religions, however, God, *by his very nature*, is omnipotent, omniscient, and perfectly good. He *cannot* become weak, ignorant, or ignoble. Just as the number 2 is necessarily even, God is necessarily supreme in power, goodness, and knowledge. He is not some infant deity who by earnest striving slowly acquired these perfections and, like us, can diminish his goodness by intentionally acting badly. He necessarily has these perfections from all eternity, and he cannot divest himself of them anymore than the number 2 can cease to be even. God's perfections are constituents of his nature, not acquired characteristics. So, while we may be free to diminish our degree of goodness by using our freedom to pursue the bad, God is not free to lose his perfections by using his freedom to pursue the bad. Indeed, he is not free to pursue the bad. For if he were free to pursue the bad, then he could become less than perfect. And that is simply impossible.

The problem of divine perfection and freedom was particularly acute for Leibniz. Since God necessarily exists and is necessarily omnipotent, omniscient, and perfectly good, it seems he necessarily would be drawn to create the best. If this were so, then when God surveyed all the possible worlds, he must have chosen the best, with the result that the actual world is the best of all possible worlds. Leibniz embraced the conclusion of this reasoning: the actual world is the best of all possible worlds. But how then could God be free in choosing to create the best? As a first step in the direction of answering this question, we should note that two quite different views of divine freedom have emerged in Western thought. According to the first view, God is free in creating a world or in acting within the world he has created provided nothing *outside* of God determines him to create the world he creates or determines him to act in a particular way in the world he has created. According to the second view, God is free in creating or acting within his creation provided it was in his power not to create what he did or not to act within his creation as he did.

The first of these two views has the advantage of establishing beyond question that God possesses freedom with respect to his selection of a world to create. For given that he is omnipotent and the creator things other than himself, it is evident that nothing *outside o* determines him to create whatever he does create. And given that whatever he creates is within his control, it would seem that he is completely at liberty to act as he sees fit within the world he has created. So, the fact that nothing outside of God determines him to create or act as he does clearly shows that God is an *autonomous* agent; he is self-determining in the sense that his actions are the result of decisions that are determined only by his own nature. But is this sufficient to establish that God is *genuinely* free? We believe that a human being may not be free in performing a certain action even when it is clear that the person was not determined to perform that action by external forces. Perhaps the person was in the grip of some internal passion or irresistible impulse that necessitated the performance of that action, overcoming the person's judgment that the action was wrong or unwise. With respect to human beings, the defender of the first view of divine freedom can agree that the mere absence of determining external agents or forces is not sufficient for an individual's action to be free. But in the case of God, as opposed to humans, the defender can argue that it is sufficient. For in God there is no possibility of his passions overcoming the judgment of reason. As Leibniz remarks:

the Stoics said that only the wise man is free; and one's mind is indeed not free when it is possessed by a great passion, for then one cannot will as one should, i.e. with proper deliberation. It is in that way that God alone is perfectly free, and the created minds are free only in proportion as they are above passion.[13]

The chief objection to this view of divine freedom is that it doesn't sufficiently recognize the importance of agents having *control* over their free acts. An action was performed freely only if the agent was free to perform the action and free not to perform it. It must have been up to the agent whether to perform or not perform that act. If some external force or internal passion was beyond the control of the agent, and the agent's action was inevitable given that external force or internal passion, then the agent did not act freely in performing that action. Since God is a purely rational being and not subject to uncontrollable passions that sometimes compel human agents to act, it is tempting to conclude that God enjoys perfect freedom of action. But this will be so only if

[13] *New Essays on Human Understanding*, trans. and ed. P. Remnant and J. Bennett (Cambridge: Cambridge University Press, 1982), 175.

there are no other features God has that both necessitate his actions and are not within his control. Because human agents are generally thought to have the power to act against the counsel of reason, we credit their acts due to reason—as opposed to those acts due to irresistible impulses—as acts they perform freely. For we believe they were free to reject the counsel of reason and act otherwise. But what if God *cannot* reject the counsel of his reason as to what action to perform? A human agent who is morally good and rational may yet have the power to refrain from acting as his goodness and reason direct. But can this be true of God? And, if it cannot be, how can we then say that God acts freely?

Leibniz was well aware of the problem posed by the fact that God's choice of the best is *necessary*, given that he is necessarily omnipotent, omniscient, and perfectly good. In fact, his most well-known solution to the problem of divine perfection and freedom recognizes that if God's choice of the best is *absolutely necessary* then God is not free with respect to creation. In his *Theodicy* and in his correspondence with Clarke, he is careful to distinguish *absolute necessity, hypothetical necessity*, and *moral necessity*, arguing that it is morally necessary but not absolutely necessary that God chose to create the best world. To determine whether Leibniz can solve the problem of divine perfection and freedom we need to examine his distinction between moral and absolute necessity and see whether he succeeds in escaping the charge that on his view of things it is *absolutely necessary* that God chooses to create the best. I shall argue that he cannot escape the charge.

In discussing this matter it will be helpful to consider the following argument.

(1) If God exists and is omnipotent, perfectly wise and good, then he chooses to create the best of all possible worlds. [That Leibniz is committed to (1) follows from (a) his view that God is determined by the best, and (b) his view that among possible worlds there is a unique best world.]

(2) God exists and is omnipotent, perfectly wise, and perfectly good. [Leibniz endorses the Ontological Argument which purports to be a proof of (2).]

therefore,

(3) God chooses to create the best of all possible worlds.

As we've noted, it is of crucial importance for Leibniz to deny that (3) is absolutely necessary. For whatever is absolutely necessary cannot logically be otherwise. Hence, if (3) is absolutely necessary, it would be logically impossible for God to choose to create any world other than the best. It would not be a contingent matter that God chooses to create the best. Nor, of course, could God be free in choosing to create the best.

Leibniz contends that God's choosing to create the best is morally necessary, not absolutely necessary. Here are several of his most pertinent remarks on this issue in his major work, *Theodicy*.

> God is bound by a moral necessity, to make things in such a manner that there can be nothing better: otherwise . . . he would not himself be satisfied with his work, he would blame himself for its imperfection; and that conflicts with the supreme felicity of the divine nature. (T, 253)

> God chose between different courses all possible: thus metaphysically speaking, he could have chosen or done what was not the best; but he could not morally speaking have done so. (T, 271)

> . . . one must confess that there is evil in this world which God has made, and that it would have been possible to make a world without evil or even not to create any world, since its creation depended upon the free will of God. (T, 378)

Leibniz's point in the last passage quoted is that God followed the best course in creating this world, even though it contains some evil. But he is careful to add that logically speaking God could have created a world without evil (albeit a less good world than the one he has created) or could have refrained from creating any world.

What is it for it to be *morally necessary* for God to choose to create the best of all possible worlds? It seems clear that its meaning is such that if we suppose that God chooses to create less than the best, or not to create at all, it would logically follow that he is lacking in wisdom, goodness, or power. Indeed, Leibniz says that 'to do less good than one could is to be lacking in wisdom or in goodness', that the most perfect understanding 'cannot fail to act in the most perfect way, and consequently to choose the best' (T, 252). Consider again proposition (1) in the above argument. What Leibniz says about moral necessity implies that (1) is itself *absolutely necessary*. For he clearly holds that from the fact that a being does less good than it could it *logically follows* that the being in question is lacking in wisdom or goodness. And one cannot hold this without being committed to holding that the consequent of (1) [he chooses to create the best of all possible worlds] *logically follows from* the antecedent of (1) [God exists and is omnipotent, perfectly wise and good].[14] That is, Leibniz is committed to holding that (1) is a *hypothetical necessity*. An if-then proposition is a hypothetical necessity provided the consequent logically follows from the antecedent.[15] [One might also say, with some loss of clarity, that the consequent is necessary on the hypothesis of the antecedent.] Of course, the mere fact that a particular consequent logically follows from a certain antecedent—as, for example, 'John is unmarried' logically follows from 'John is a bachelor'—is insufficient to render the consequent *absolutely necessary*. It is not logically impossible for 'John is unmarried' to be false. So, although his asserting the moral necessity of God's choosing to create the best commits Leibniz to the absolute necessity of the hypothetical proposition (1), in itself this commitment still leaves him free to deny that God's choosing to create the best is absolutely necessary. Two further points show that he cannot escape the conclusion that God's choosing to create the best is absolutely necessary. First, proposition (2) [God exists and is omnipotent, perfectly wise, and perfectly good], the antecedent of (1), is itself absolutely necessary. We've already noted that both Clarke and Leibniz are committed to the view that (2) is not a contingent truth; it is absolutely necessary. Second, it is a rule of logic that if a hypothetical proposition is itself absolutely necessary, and its antecedent is also absolutely necessary, then its consequent must be absolutely necessary as well. Thus, if both (1) and (2) are absolutely necessary, (3) must be absolutely necessary as well. Since Leibniz is committed to the view that both (1) and (2) are absolutely necessary, we are bound to conclude that his view commits him to the view that (3) is absolutely necessary.[16]

Before turning to Clarke's attempt to solve the problem of divine perfection and freedom, there are two other issues concerning Leibniz's view that require discussion. First, we should note that Leibniz often

[14] Actually, the consequent of (1) logically follows from the antecedent of (1) only if it is absolutely necessary that there is a best possible world. Leibniz does think it is absolutely necessary that there is a unique best among possible worlds.

[15] It is also true that a proposition q logically follows from another proposition p just in case the hypothetical proposition, if p then q, is absolutely necessary.

[16] The early Leibniz toyed with denying the logical rule that what logically follows from what is absolutely necessary is itself absolutely necessary. For a scholarly and philosophically illuminating account of Leibniz's various efforts to avoid the conclusion we've reached, see Robert Adam's *Leibniz: Determinist, Theist, Idealist* (Oxford: Oxford University Press, 1994), ch. 1.

insists that the act of will must be free in the sense of not b\
necessitated by the motives that give rise to it. His remark on this mat\
(often repeated) is that motives 'incline without necessitating' (LC, 5\)
This view *appears* to conflict with the view I have ascribed to him: that
the strongest motive in the agent *determines* the agent to choose as
he does. It suggests instead that the agent had the power to will otherwise even though the motive and circumstances be unchanged. For, as
he says, the motives don't necessitate but only incline the agent to will
as he does. But this is not what he means by his phrase 'motives incline
without necessitating'. On his view, motives and circumstances necessitate the act of will in the sense that it is logically or causally impossible
that those motives and circumstances should obtain and the act of
will not occur. Leibniz's claim that they don't necessitate the act of will
means only that the act of will *itself* is not thereby rendered something
that is absolutely necessary.[17] That is, he is simply noting that even
though there be a necessary connection between the motive and the
act of will, this does not mean that the act of will cannot *itself* be
contingent. As we saw above, God's being omnipotent, omniscient, and
perfectly good *necessitates* God's choice of the best. However, the fact
that there is a necessary connection between his being perfect and his
choice of the best does not imply that his choice of the best is itself
absolutely necessary. Leibniz registers this point (in a somewhat mislead-
ing fashion) by saying that God's motives 'incline without necessitating'
his choice of the best. We must not be misled by this phrase into
thinking that he holds that the *connection* between his being perfect
and his choice of the best is anything less than absolutely necessary.
And when we then note, as we have, that God's being perfect is
absolutely necessary, the logical rule dictates the conclusion that his
choice of the best is itself absolutely necessary. This being so, we can
conclude that God's choice to create the best is not free; it is absolutely
necessary.

The second issue concerns the first premiss of our argument to show
that Leibniz is committed to the absolute necessity of (3) [God chooses
to create the best of all possible worlds]. As we saw, Leibniz's views
commit him to the absolute necessity of (1) [If God exists and is

---

[17] For a more extended account of this interpretation of Leibniz's dictum, 'motives incline
but do not necessitate', see G. H. R. Parkinson, *Leibniz on Human Freedom* (Wiesbaden: Franz
Steiner Verlag, 1970), 50–3.

omnipotent, perfectly wise and good, then he chooses to create the best of all possible worlds]. But a serious question can be raised about (1). For the conjunction of the proposition that God exists and (1) implies that among the possible worlds God surveys there is one that is the best, a world than which none better is possible. And many philosophers have doubted that there is such a world. Indeed, as we have noted, some philosophers follow Aquinas in arguing that for any world whatever there is a world better than it. How then can Leibniz show that there is a best world among possible worlds?[18] Although this is a perplexing and complicated matter, it is not too difficult to see a line of reasoning Leibniz might have followed. As Blumenthal notes in his important essay on this issue,[19] Leibniz appeals to two principles in his reasoning about what God would create: the Principle of Sufficient Reason (PSR), and the Principle of the Best (PB). According to PSR, God has a sufficient reason for any act he performs. Leibniz held that PSR is a *necessary* truth. According to PB, God never prefers the less perfect to the more perfect. Leibniz's official position is that PB is in itself a *contingent* truth. Reporting Leibniz's official position, Blumenthal remarks:

... Leibniz holds that the fact that God is determined by the best (the principle of perfection) is contingent—being itself a matter of free choice. It is, strictly speaking, possible that God should choose less than the best, though it is *certain* that he will not. Leibniz's motives for holding this view are clear: he wishes to preserve God's freedom and avoid the charge that this world is the only one that is (really) possible. How God's choice of the best can be contingent, given that he is by definition all-good, is a serious and well-known problem.[20]

I've argued above that given God's necessary perfections and necessary existence, the 'serious and well-known problem' to which Blumenthal alludes can have only one outcome: despite Leibniz's claims to the contrary, it is logically impossible for Leibniz's God to prefer less than the best. God's preference for the best is necessary, not contingent. If this is right, Leibniz's principles commit him to the *necessity* of God's not preferring or choosing the less perfect instead of the more perfect.

---

[18] The question here is not whether there is a best possible world, but whether the basic philosophical principles to which Leibniz appeals enable him to deduce the existence of a best possible world.

[19] David Blumenthal, 'Is the Best Possible World Possible?', *Philosophical Review* 84/2 (Apr. 1975), 163–77.

[20] Ibid. 169.

Taking PB, no less than PSR, as a *necessary* truth, let's now consider how PSR and PB support Leibniz's view that there is a best possible world. What is needed is a proof that on the alternatives to there being a best world—(a) for any world there is a better world, (b) there is more than one world that is as good as any other world—God would not create a world at all. For, since we know that there is an actual world and that in Leibniz's philosophy God necessarily exists and must have created that world, any proof that if either (a) or (b) were true God would not have created a world at all, suffices to show that the world God has created is in fact the best possible world.[21]

Suppose that (a) is true, that for any world there is a world that is better than it. Clearly, God could not then choose to create any world. For to choose to create a particular world would be to prefer something less good than another world—a violation of PB. Does God then *choose* not to create any world? No, for a good world is better than no world at all. And God will always make the best choice or no choice at all. So, God's not creating a world does not require his actually *choosing* not to create. As Blumenthal notes, while Leibniz's God would have an overall preference to create rather than not, he would not have a sufficient reason to create any particular world, given that for any world there is a better. Since there is an actual world, God has created that world and had a sufficient reason to do so. Therefore, it cannot be that for any world God could create there is a better he could create instead.

What of alternative (b)—although there is no unique best world, there are several worlds that are equally good, and none better? Here God could create a world without thereby failing to create a better world. So, in creating one of the best worlds God would not be violating PB. The problem is that he would have no sufficient reason to create the one he does, rather than any of the others that are equally good. Thus God would violate PSR, he would lack a sufficient reason for creating the world that he does rather than some other equally good world. So, again, God would not create any world at all. But again, his not creating any world would not be a *choice* he makes. It is the result of his not having a sufficient reason to choose any particular world to create. In sum, as Leibniz says, 'In my opinion, if there were no best possible series,

<hr />

[21] Given the evils we know to exist, the idea that the world we live in is the best possible world seems an absurd idea. Leibniz, however, argued that the evils in our world actually contribute to the goodness of the whole of which they are a part.

God would have certainly created nothing, since he cannot act without a reason, or prefer the less perfect to the more perfect.'[22]

Given the above results, as Blumenthal points out, a simple argument is available by which Leibniz can prove that among possible worlds there is a best world. Since God exists and there is an actual world he has created, that world must be the best possible world. For otherwise God could not have created it. But if the actual world is the best possible world, then certainly there is a best world among possible worlds.[23]

---

[22] *Leibniz Selections*, ed. Wiener, 95.

[23] Blumenthal does not endorse the conclusion I've reached, for he works only within the framework of Leibniz's 'official' position that PB is contingent.

2

Clarke on Divine Perfection and Freedom

In contrast to Locke, who characterized freedom as the power to carry out the *action* that we choose (will) to do, leaving the choice (volition) itself to be causally necessitated by the agent's motives, Clarke locates freedom squarely at the level of the *choice* to act or not act: '...the essence of liberty consists in (a person's) having a continual power of choosing whether he shall act or whether he shall forbear acting' (D, 101). The implication of Clarke's view is that freedom (liberty) would be impossible should a person's choices be causally necessitated by his motives or desires. For if a person's choice to act is causally necessitated by earlier states of his body or mind, then at the time of that choice it was not in the agent's power to choose to not act. It is for Clarke a secondary matter whether the agent is able to carry out his choice.[1] Of course, since God is omnipotent, his power to carry out the action he chooses to do is unlimited. But our question is whether God has it in his power to *choose to refrain* from following what he knows to be the best course of action. Should he lack that power, it follows from Clarke's conception of freedom that God does not *freely choose* the best course of action. In fact, it would follow for Clarke that in this instance God is totally passive and not an agent at all. It would also follow for Clarke that it would make no sense to praise or thank God for choosing the best course of action. We must now see how Clarke endeavors to

---

[1] Clarke goes so far as to declare that a prisoner in chains is free to will to leave or will to stay. That he cannot successfully execute his choice doesn't rob him of the power to choose (D, 101). (Of course, he would allow that one who knows he is in chains may well see the pointlessness of choosing to leave and, therefore, not exercise his power so to choose.)

avoid the absolute necessity of God's choosing in accordance with his knowledge of what is the best course of action.

Clarke's overall view is clear enough. He distinguishes between the intellect (understanding) and the will. It is the function of the understanding to determine what course of action to pursue. It is the function of the will (the power we have to will this or that) to initiate the action specified by the understanding. It is one thing, however, to arrive (through deliberation) at the judgment that doing a certain thing is best,[2] and quite another thing to choose (will) to do that thing. Often enough, our motives and desires are sufficiently clear and strong to causally necessitate the judgment as to what to do. No other judgment is possible in the circumstances. In short, there may be no freedom at all with respect to the *judgment* as to what action to perform. On Clarke's view, freedom enters only when the will chooses to act, or not act, in accordance with the judgment of the understanding. Thus, when there is a best course of action for God to perform, his judgment that it is the best course to pursue is, Clarke tells us, *absolutely necessary.*[3] But God's choice to act in accordance with what his understanding approves is completely free; he always has the power to choose otherwise.

God always discerns and approves what is just and good, necessarily, and cannot do otherwise: But he always acts or does what is just and good freely; that is, having at the same time a full natural or physical power of acting differently.[4]

It is instructive to contrast Clarke's view of freedom with a stream of thought in Christian theology, dating back at least to Augustine, according to which the saints in heaven are perfected to the degree that they not only do not sin, they no longer are *able* to sin, a perfection that is found in God and the angels. In our earthly state we have the freedom to turn from the good and do evil, but in the life to come we

---

[2] Since such a judgment terminates the process of deliberation about what to do, Clarke and others referred to it as 'the last judgment of the understanding'. It is the judgment that terminates deliberation and is followed by the act of will to perform (or not perform) the action specified in the judgment.

[3] Clarke uses several different expressions to designate the sort of necessity that precludes freedom to do otherwise. His favorite expressions are 'physical necessity' and 'natural necessity'. But he also uses 'absolute necessity' on occasion. And in his fifth letter in response to Leibniz he says: '*Necessity,* in philosophical questions, always signifies absolute necessity' (LC, 99).

[4] Answer to the third Letter, 12 Jan. 1716–17, in Clarke, *Works* (Garland edn.), iv. 717.

shall have a superior sort of freedom,[5] a freedom that does not includ
the *ability* to do evil. Thus Augustine says:

For the first freedom of will which man received when he was created upright
consisted in an ability not to sin, but also in an ability to sin; whereas this last
freedom of will shall be superior, inasmuch as it shall not be able to sin. This,
indeed, shall not be a natural ability, but the gift of God. For it is one thing to be
God, another thing to be a partaker of God. God by nature cannot sin, but the
partaker of God receives this inability from God.[6]

In his book, *A Philosophical Inquiry Concerning Human Liberty*, Anthony
Collins had appealed to this stream of thought in support of his view that
freedom does not require any power to choose or do otherwise. Clarke
wrote a rather devastating response to Collins's book. In the course of
his response to Collins we find the following remark:

Neither saints, nor angels, nor God himself, have in any degree the less liberty
upon account of the perfection of their nature: Because between the *physical
power of action* and the *perfection of judgment* which is not action (which two things
this author constantly confounds) there is no connection. God judges what is
right, and approves what is good, by a physical necessity of nature; in which
physical necessity, all notion of action is necessarily excluded. But *doing* what is
good is wholly owing to an active principle, in which is essentially included the
notion of liberty.[7]

Clearly, Clarke rejects this stream of thought in Christian theology. He
allows that the saints in heaven no longer have any desire to sin and take
no delight in it. Indeed, it may be absolutely certain that with purified
desires and a perfected judgment they will always *freely* do what is right.[8]
And this will be an enormous difference from life on earth where we are
often tempted to sin by bad desires and faulty judgment. But what
cannot be is that the saints or the angels, or God for that matter, cease
to have the *ability* or *power* to choose to do other than what is right. For
then they would not be free in choosing and doing what is right. To lose
the power to choose otherwise is to lose the power to choose freely. And
if one loses that power one ceases to be an agent at all.

---

[5] Not all of us, of course. Only those who have seen the light and have been granted
eternal salvation.

[6] *The City of God*, bk. 22, ch. 30.

[7] *Dr. Clarke's Remarks upon a Book entitled A Philosophical Enquiry Concerning Human Liberty*,
in Clarke, *Works* (Garland edn.), iv. 731.

[8] See D, 124 for his clear statement of this view.

We can begin to get at the difficulty in Clarke's view of divine freedom by considering God's perfections and their implications for whether he *can* freely choose to do *evil*. Clarke readily sees that were a perfectly good, omniscient being to freely choose to do some evil deed, it would thereby cease to be perfectly good. And it would cease to be perfectly good even if, as could not happen in God's case, it were prevented from carrying out the evil deed it chose to do. For the free choice to do evil is *itself* inconsistent with continuing to be a perfectly good, omniscient being. A being who freely chooses to do what it *knows* to be an evil deed thereby ceases to be a perfectly good being. So, if God were to freely choose to do an evil deed, he would cease to be perfectly good. In short, it is not logically possible for God both to freely choose to do evil *and* to continue to be perfectly good. Now, since Clarke holds with Leibniz that God *necessarily* exists and *necessarily* is omnipotent, omniscient, and perfectly good,[9] we can advance to the simpler conclusion that it is not logically possible for God to freely choose to do evil. It is not logically possible because it is inconsistent with what is logically necessary: the existence of a being (God) who is necessarily omnipotent, omniscient, and perfectly good.

Consider now the question: Does God ever freely choose *not* to do evil? I think we can see that Clarke's own views commit him to a negative answer to this question. For God chooses freely *not* to do something only if it is in his power to choose to do that thing—choosing freely, Clarke insists, logically requires the power to choose otherwise. But it cannot be in anyone's power to make a certain choice if it is logically impossible that the person make that choice.[10] Therefore, since it is logically impossible for God to choose to do evil, it is not in God's power to choose to do evil. And since it is not in God's power to choose to do evil, it cannot be that God's choice not to do evil is a *free* choice. If God chooses not to do evil, he so chooses of necessity, not freely. And this being so, it makes no sense for us to thank God, or to be grateful to him, for choosing not to do evil. He could not have chosen otherwise.

Since the claim that God does not *freely* choose not to do evil is rather central to my examination of Clarke's views on divine perfection and

---

[9] An *essential* attribute of a being is an attribute that the being *necessarily* possesses. Clarke holds that the moral perfections of the deity are *essential* aspects of the divine nature: '...justice, goodness, and all the other moral attributes of God are as *essential* to the divine nature as the natural attributes of eternity, infinity, and the like' (D, 120).

[10] If there is no possible world in which a person makes a certain choice, it cannot be that the person, nevertheless, has it within his power to make that choice.

freedom, I want to advance another argument in support of it, one that I find particularly compelling.

1. If p logically implies q, and q is false, it is in an agent's power to bring it about that p only if it is in that agent's power to bring it about that q.[11]
2. That God chooses to do evil logically implies that God is not perfectly good.
3. It is false that God is not perfectly good.

therefore,

4. If it is in God's power to bring it about that he chooses to do evil then it is in his power to bring it about that he is not perfectly good. (from 1, 2, and 3)
5. It is not in God's power to bring it about that he is not perfectly good.[12]

therefore,

6. It is not in God's power to choose to do evil.

therefore,

7. If God chooses not to do evil, God chooses not to do evil of necessity, not freely.

Before turning to what I regard as two attempts by Clarke to avoid any limitations on the scope of divine liberty, we should consider whether it is in God's power to choose contrary to what he judges to be best. We've concluded that God cannot choose to do evil. But to choose contrary to what is judged to be best is evil or morally wrong only if choosing to do what is judged to be best is morally obligatory. To claim that it is morally obligatory ignores the real possibility that choosing what is best is supererogatory, beyond the call of duty. There are choices which are good to make but not required as our duty. It would be a mistake, therefore, to infer God's inability to choose to act contrary to what he judges to be best from his inability to choose to do evil. Nevertheless, it

---

[11] For a discussion and defense of this principle see my essay 'Fatalism and Truth', *Southern Journal of Philosophy*, 18 (1980), 213–19. For a fuller discussion of this principle and others see William Hasker's *God, Time, and Knowledge* (Ithaca, NY: Cornell University Press, 1989), 96–115.

[12] God necessarily exists and is necessarily perfectly good. Therefore, it cannot be in his power to bring it about that he does not exist or that he is not perfectly good. Just as the number 2 cannot cease to be even, God cannot cease to be perfectly good.

does seem to be logically impossible for perfect goodness to choose to act contrary to what is best. And this seems to be Clarke's own view of the matter. Thus he declares 'that though God is a most perfectly *free* agent, yet he cannot but do always what is *best* and *wisest* in the whole' (D, 120–1). To choose otherwise, he thinks, is to act contrary to perfect wisdom and goodness.

How does Clarke endeavor to avoid the conclusion that God's perfect goodness precludes his being free in many of his choices? His general approach to this difficulty is to distinguish two sorts of necessities: *moral* and *physical*. If one state or event physically necessitates another state or event, then the second state or event cannot occur freely. Thus he would say that hanging a greater weight on the left end of an accurate balance physically necessitates the downward movement on the left side of the balance. Here, even if the balance were endowed with consciousness, there would be no possibility of the balance freely moving downward on the left. For the balance has no power to do other than move downwards on the left side. To illustrate the other sort of necessity, he offers the example of God's promising that on a given day he will not destroy the world. The promise morally necessitates God's refraining from destroying the world on that particular day. But, says Clarke, it would be absurd to think that God therefore lacked the physical power on that day to destroy the world.[13] God's refraining from destroying the world on that day is both morally necessary and free. For he both retains the physical power to destroy the world on that day and also cannot (morally speaking) break his promise.

One difficulty with this solution is that it doesn't focus on the particular act of God's *choosing* to break his promise. Instead, Clarke focuses on what would be the *result* of choosing to break his promise— God's exertion of his physical power on that day to destroy the world. Because God *cannot* choose to break his solemn promise, there is no need to deny to him the physical power to destroy the world on that day. A being can have the physical power to perform an act, even if that being cannot perform that act owing to his not being able to *choose* to perform that act. A loving grandfather undoubtedly possesses the physical power

---

[13] 'God's performing his promise is always consequent upon his making it: Yet there is *no connection* between them, as between cause and effect: For, not the promise of God, but his active power, is the alone physical or efficient cause of the performance.' See *Dr. Clarke's Remarks upon a Book entitled A Philosophical Enquiry Concerning Human Liberty*, in Clarke, *Works* (Garland edn.), iv. 9.

to cause the death of his 5-year-old granddaughter by choking her. But it may well not be in his power to perform that action simply because it is not in his power to bring himself to intentionally choose to kill her. The real question for Clarke here is not whether God has the physical power to destroy the world on any particular day—he surely does. It is whether having given his solemn promise not to destroy the world on a given day it is, nevertheless, in his power to *choose* effectively to destroy the world on that day. If we accept, as it seems we must in God's case, that it is logically impossible for God to *choose* to break his solemn promise on that day, then it follows that it is not in God's power to break his solemn promise on that day. That it is not in God's power to so choose is due to the fact that such a choice would amount to divesting himself of his absolute perfection. And, clearly, it is not logically possible for God to cease to be absolutely perfect.

In a revealing passage Clarke appears to recognize that there are some choices that do not lie within God's power because they logically imply the destruction of his essential perfections. He begins the passage by noting that there are necessary relations among states of affairs, relations that God eternally knows. By this he means that some states of things are *necessarily better than* other states of things. (For example, *there being innocent beings who do not suffer eternally* is necessarily better than *there being innocent beings who do suffer eternally*.) By knowing these necessary relations, God knows the choices required by his perfect wisdom and goodness. Noting that God cannot but choose to act always according to this knowledge, he continues:

It being as truly impossible for such a free agent, who is absolutely incapable of being deceived or depraved, to choose, by acting contrary to these laws, to destroy its own *perfections*; as for *necessary existence to be able to destroy its own being*. (D, 122)

He then draws the obvious conclusion that

From hence it follows, that though God is both perfectly *free* and infinitely *powerful*, yet he cannot possibly do any thing that is *evil*. The reason of this also is evident. Because, as it is manifest infinite power cannot extend to natural contradictions, which imply a destruction of that very power by which they must be supposed to be elected; so neither can it extend to moral contradictions, which imply a destruction of some other attributes, as necessarily belonging to the divine nature as power. I have already shown that justice, goodness and truth are necessarily in God; even as necessarily as power, understanding, and knowledge of the nature of things. It is therefore as impossible and contradictory to suppose his will should choose to do any thing contrary to justice, goodness, or truth; as that his power should be able to do any thing inconsistent with power. (D, 122)

The conclusion I draw from these remarks is that God's liberty is curtailed by his perfect goodness. If choosing to do something rules out his being perfectly good, then it is not in his power to choose to do that thing. He necessarily, not freely, chooses *not* to do that thing. This is the conclusion we argued for above. Clarke, however, rejects this conclusion, insisting instead that God's liberty is not in the least diminished.

It is no diminution of power not to be able to do things which are no object of power. And it is in like manner no diminution either of power or liberty to have such a perfect and unalterable rectitude of will as never possibly to *choose* to do anything inconsistent with that rectitude. (D, 122)

Our final question is whether Clarke can successfully defend this response. As is clear, the response depends on an analogy between being perfectly powerful (omnipotent) and being perfectly free. His argument can be understood as follows. There are some things God cannot do. He cannot make a square circle. Nor can he choose to do evil. In the first case, his making a square circle is impossible because the idea of a square circle is contradictory. In the second case, the contradiction is in the idea of a being who is necessarily perfectly good choosing to do evil. Since a contradiction is involved in each case, God's power is held to extend neither to making a square circle nor to choosing to do evil. For God's power extends only to what is not contradictory for a necessarily perfect being to do. Clarke then claims that the fact that God's power does not extend to making a square circle or choosing to do evil does not imply any diminution of power. And by analogy he infers that it does not imply any diminution of liberty in God.

Suppose we agree that God's inability to choose to do evil is not a diminution of power. Can it also be true that his inability to choose to do evil is not a diminution of freedom? I don't think so. Remember, on Clarke's account of the nature of freedom, the power to choose otherwise is *necessary* for a choice to be free. Therefore, if it is not in God's power to choose to do evil, God does not freely choose not to do evil. And if it is not in God's power to intentionally act contrary to what is best, God does not freely choose to do what is best. Perhaps Clarke can save God's omnipotence by saying that his power does not extend to acts inconsistent with any of his essential attributes. But this won't leave his perfect freedom intact. So long as he lacks the power to choose to do evil, he lacks freedom in choosing not to do evil. And so long as he lacks the power to choose contrary to what is best, he lacks freedom in choosing to do what is best. It won't matter whether this lack of power results from a deficiency in his power or from the fact that his power does not extend to such choices. Clarke might be able to patch this up by changing his account of the nature of freedom: declaring instead that one chooses freely just in case one has *the power to choose otherwise provided one's power extends to the choice to do otherwise.* This move will avoid the immediate conclusion that God does not *freely* choose to do the best. For Clarke holds that God's infinite power does not extend to choosing contrary to what he knows to be best. But since God's choosing to do what is best is *absolutely necessary* for God, we are left with no reason at all to insist that his choice is really free. Nor are we left with any reason to thank God or be grateful to him for choosing and acting in accordance with his knowledge of what is best. I conclude that Clarke's valiant effort to reconcile God's perfect liberty with his perfect goodness is unsuccessful.

We've seen that Clarke's view of what it is for an agent to be free with respect to the choice to do X is for the agent to have the power to choose to do X and the power to choose not to do X. As he says: 'the essence of liberty consists in having a continual power of choosing whether he shall act or whether he shall forbear acting.' And the difficulty we have come to with respect to God's freedom is that it is *impossible* for God to choose to do evil. And that means that God does not freely choose not to do evil. Similarly, since Clarke appears to hold with Leibniz that when there is a best for God to do, it is impossible for God to choose not to do what he sees is the best for him to do, God's perfection, as it were, logically requires God to choose to do the best. And since his so choosing is free only if he has the power to choose not to do what he sees is the best for him to do, God necessarily, not freely, chooses to do what he sees as the best. And this in turn implies, so I've contended, that we have no reason to thank God or praise God for doing what is best. For in thanking and praising an agent for doing something we presuppose that it was in the agent's power not to do that thing.

Although the difficulty just noted is intrinsic to Clarke's account of divine freedom, it can be avoided by refining the view of agent-causation advanced by Clarke. Clarke views agent-causation as the power an agent has to *choose* to do X and to *choose* to refrain from doing X. For reasons we need not pursue here, this view of agent-causation gives rise to several difficulties, only one of which has been noted in the previous paragraph. While Clarke clearly sees that agent-causation involves attributing causal power to an agent, he identifies that causal power with the agent's power to choose to do X and her power to choose to refrain from doing X. A more sophisticated view of agent-causation appeared a few decades later in the eighteenth century in the work of Thomas Reid.[14] Reid identified agent-causation with the power to cause (and the power not to cause) a volition. So, like Clarke, Reid held that agent-causation involves a power to cause a volition (choice). But he did not also require, as Clarke did, a power to cause the opposite choice (the choice to refrain from doing X). Nor did Reid require a power to cause the non-occurrence of the volition one causes. He required only the power *not to cause* that volition.[15] So, for Reid, freedom involves the power to cause a volition to do X and the power *not to cause* the volition to do X. Freedom does not also include the power to cause the volition not to do X. If a person exercises her power to cause the choice to do X, while having the power not to have caused that choice, then, for Reid, that person is free with respect to that choice (and the action initiated by the choice) and may be responsible both for choice and the action of which it is a part.

An example will help us see both the plausibility of Reid's account of a free decision and the difference between his account and Clarke's account. Smith is deliberating about killing Jones. Smith has it in his power to kill Jones—Jones is present in the room with Smith and there is a loaded gun within Smith's reach. Let us suppose that the Devil is also interested in Jones going on to his reward, but rather than killing Jones himself, would like him to die at Smith's hand. Of course, he could simply force Smith to pick up a gun and kill Jones, or he could make changes in Smith's brain so that Smith cannot stop himself from killing Jones. But then he, the Devil, would be responsible for Jones's death. And Smith would not be killing Jones of his own free will. Let us suppose that the Devil prefers that Smith do the deed of his own free will. So, the

---

[14] See Reid's *Essays on the Active Powers of Man*, vol. ii in *The Works of Thomas Reid, D.D.* (8th edn.), ed. Sir William Hamilton (Edinburgh, 1895; repr. Georg Olms Verlag, 1983).

[15] Evidence for this account of Reid's view of agent-causation is presented in my essay, 'The Metaphysics of Freedom: Reid's Theory of Agent Causation', *American Catholic Philosophical Quarterly*, 74/3 (2000) 425–46.

Devil monitors Smith's thinking about the matter and sees that Smith is on the verge of reaching a decision to kill Jones. Indeed, Smith has reached the very moment of decision. The Devil watches closely the decision process unfolding in Smith's brain, and resolves that if Smith does not complete the decision process by choosing on his own to kill Jones, he (the Devil) will directly intervene and cause Smith to make that choice by directly causing the required changes in his brain.[16] As it happens, Smith decides all on his own to kill Jones and does so, without the Devil having to take any action in the matter. Here, we may judge, and, I believe, judge rightly, that Smith freely decided to kill Jones and did so as a result of that decision. Or, at least, nothing in our story gives us reason to judge otherwise. But we should note that while Reid's account of a free decision is satisfied in this case, Clarke's is not. Reid's account is satisfied because on his own Smith caused his decision to kill Jones and had the power *not to cause* that decision. Of course, had Smith not caused his decision to kill Jones, he would have decided to kill Jones anyway—but not by virtue of *his causing* that decision. For had he not caused that decision, the Devil, and not Smith, would have caused Smith's decision to kill Jones. And had the Devil done so with the result that Smith decides to kill Jones, he, Smith, would not be responsible for that decision because the Devil, and not Smith, caused him to decide to kill Jones. But on Clarke's account of a free decision the outcome is different. Again, Smith decides on his own to kill Jones and does so. But since, owing to the Devil and his resolve, Smith did not have the power to cause the opposite decision—the decision not to kill Jones—Clarke's account implies that in this case Smith did not freely choose to kill Jones and, therefore, was not responsible for doing so.

Suppose, then, that we replace Clarke's account of agent-causation with Reid's more sophisticated account whereby a person is the agent-cause of his decision to do X provided he caused that decision and had the power not to cause it. Will this enable us to say that God is free with respect to his decision not to do evil? And, assuming with Clarke and Leibniz that there is a best course of action for God to pursue, will Reid's account enable us to say that God is free with respect to his decision to do what he sees is the best course of action? An affirmative answer on

---

[16] This example duplicates the main point made by an example in Harry G. Frankfurt's well-known essay 'Alternative Possibilities and Moral Responsibility', *Journal of Philosophy,* 66 (1969), 829–39.

Reid's behalf will not be subject to the complaint that it must then be in God's power to decide to do evil, or in his power to decide not to pursue the best course of action. For, as we've seen, Reid's account of a free decision requires only that the agent cause her decision while having the power not to cause it. Thus, God's being free (on Reid's account) in deciding to pursue the best course of action requires only that it be in his power to cause that decision and in his power not to cause it. But can it be in God's power *not* to cause a decision which he knows to be the best decision he could make? In a technical sense it seems it could. For we can imagine that among the decisions for courses of action available to God there may be one that is better than any other decision. But perhaps not causing that decision (or any other decision for a course of action) is better yet. Sometimes not doing anything is better than doing any of the things one can do. For example, if God's choice in creating a world were limited to bad worlds, then his not causing a decision to create a world would be better than his causing the decision to create, say, the least bad of the bad worlds. But surely God's power is not limited to bad choices. So, it must be true that there are good choices God can cause himself to make that are better than his not causing any choice at all. And what if, as Leibniz supposes and Clarke is at least willing to countenance, there is a best possible world that God can create. Is it in God's power *not* to create that world? It must be on Reid's view of freedom, if God was free to create that world. For on Reid's view, power to cause implies power not to cause. So, if it was in God's power to create the best possible world, it was in his power not to create it. But can it be in God's power *not* to create the best possible world? Does God have the power to cause himself not to create the best possible world? If we say that he does, then, for him to exercise that power would be for him to decide not to create the best world.[17] But is it consistent with God's absolute perfection that he decides not to create the best world, choosing in effect to produce less good than he can, or perhaps no good at all? Clearly, there is something profoundly right in Leibniz's remark that 'to do less good than one could is to be lacking in wisdom or in goodness'. And it makes little difference if we modify the remark to read 'to deliberately refrain from doing what one sees as the best is to be lacking in wisdom or in goodness'. And this

---

[17] Since nothing can prevent God from causing or not causing a decision to create or a decision not to create, God's exercising his power not to create the best world amounts to his causing his decision not to create the best world.

last (deliberately refraining from doing what one sees as the best) is what God would be doing if he exercised his power not to create the best world. If doing less good that one could is to be lacking in wisdom or goodness, surely deliberately doing nothing as opposed to doing what is best is also to be lacking in wisdom or goodness. So, even on Reid's sophisticated understanding of what it is to have power to cause or not cause, the conclusion seems inevitable: if there is a best world, God is not free not to will to bring it into being.

In this chapter and the last we have begun our exploration of the problem of divine perfection and freedom by examining the views of two important eighteenth-century philosophers, Gottfried Leibniz and Samuel Clarke. In each case we've encountered imaginative, insightful efforts to solve this problem in a manner that allows for the consistency of perfect goodness and genuine freedom in God. I have argued that neither solution succeeds in reaching that goal. If my arguments are successful, this failure should be seen more as an indication of the intractable nature of the problem of divine perfection and freedom than as a reflection on the philosophical brilliance of either Clarke or Leibniz. We also noted that the problem did not go away, but only resurfaced, when we moved from Clarke's account of agent-causation to Reid's somewhat more sophisticated account. So long as we allow that there is a best possible world and that, as Leibniz proclaims, 'to do less good than one could is to be lacking in wisdom and goodness', there appears to be no escape from the conclusion that God does not enjoy freedom with respect to creation. He was not free not to create. And he was not free to create any world other than the best possible world.

3

Aquinas and the Infinity of Possible Worlds

On the assumption that among the possible worlds there is a best world, we have considered at some length the alternatives facing God as creator. And we have reached the preliminary conclusion that God's absolute perfection would leave him no choice other than the choice to create the very best world. Were it settled that among possible worlds there is a best world, we could now press on with our study of philosophical objections to our preliminary conclusion that God is not free with respect to creation. But there is a long tradition among religious thinkers in the West that opposes the Leibnizian view that there is a best possible world. If this tradition has it right, there is no problem about God's freedom with respect to creating a world other than the best. For there simply is no best possible world for God to consider creating. Among important historical figures who hold this view, the medieval philosopher and theologian Thomas Aquinas (1225–74) exercised great influence on the development of philosophical theology in the West. So we can do no better than to consider some of his reasons for denying that there is a best possible world. In addition, in light of the number of philosophers who agree with Aquinas on this point, we must consider the implications of Aquinas's view for our basic question of whether God can be free with respect to creation.

In an important and influential study of Aquinas's views on creation, Norman Kretzmann divides those views into those addressing what he sees to be the *general* problem of creation and those addressing what he sees to be the *particular* problem of creation.[1] By the general problem of creation Kretzmann means the problem of answering the question: Why would God, the absolutely perfect being, create anything at all? After all, being absolutely perfect, it is not as though God has any *need* for anything other than himself. So, why would God create anything? The second problem, the one that will be the main focus of our discussion, is the problem of answering the question of why God would create this particular world, rather than some other world. To the first question Aquinas gives a simple, straightforward answer: God creates to manifest his goodness. 'Moreover, the communication of being and goodness arises from goodness. This is evident from the very nature and definition of the good.'[2] Several lines later he says '... the good is diffusive of itself and of being. But this diffusion befits God because ... God is the cause of being for other things.'[3] The difficulty with viewing God's creation of some world or other as a free act is that God's goodness is a necessary aspect of his nature, and if goodness is necessarily 'diffusive of itself' then it would seem to be necessary that God express his goodness in creating some world or another. Kretzmann, himself, thinks that this line of reasoning is successful. He expresses his own view on the general problem of creation by concluding

that God's goodness requires things other than itself as a manifestation of itself, that God therefore necessarily (though freely) wills the creation of something or other, and that the free choice involved in creation is confined to the selection of which possibilities to actualize for the purpose of manifesting goodness.[4]

As Kretzmann notes, however, Aquinas denies that God's goodness requires him to create some world or other, maintaining that God was free not to create anything at all. But putting this *general* problem aside until later in this chapter, the question we need to answer is whether the

---

[1] See 'A General Problem of Creation' and 'A Particular Problem of Creation' in Scott MacDonald (ed.), *Being and Goodness: The Concept of the Good in Metaphysics and Philosophical Theology* (Ithaca, NY Cornell University Press, 1991), 208–49.

[2] *Summa contra Gentiles*, lib. 1, d. 37.

[3] Ibid. The expression 'the good is diffusive of itself and being' is due to pseudo-Dionysius, the fifth- or sixth-century author of Christian Neoplatonist writings which at the time of Aquinas were still mistakenly thought to have been authored by the Dionysius mentioned in the Bible (Acts 17: 34) as having been converted by St Paul. Aquinas and others in the medieval period viewed his writings as having special importance.

[4] 'A Particular Problem of Creation', 229.

world God does create must be, as Leibniz contended, the best possible world. And on this question Aquinas very clearly gives a negative answer. For he appears to hold that there simply cannot be any such world. Although Kretzmann argues in support of Aquinas's view on the *particular* problem of creation, he thinks that most philosophers who have considered the issue hold with Leibniz that since God is omniscient, omnipotent, and perfectly good, 'he must create the best of all possible worlds if he creates anything at all'.[5] Why then does Aquinas claim otherwise?

Aquinas views a world (a universe) as consisting of *parts* in a certain *order*. And he holds that given the parts of the universe, God could not have placed the parts in a better order. The image he uses with respect to order is the relative tautness of the strings on the lute. 'For one part to be improved out of recognition would spoil the proportions of the whole design; overstretch one lute-string and the melody is lost.'[6] So, he sees the various parts of the universe as placed by God in the very best order, given those particular parts. And he claims that were a particular part to be replaced by a better part, that would disrupt the order among the parts. To continue his analogy, perhaps a given string among the strings on the lute would produce a better sound if it were stretched more tightly, or perhaps a given string could be replaced by a different string with a slightly different, but better sound. But the result, when all the strings are plucked at once may well be a less harmonious sound. Thus far, then, Aquinas appears to hold that while the universe might have had better parts, it could not be a better universe given its particular parts with their particular degrees of perfection. For God has arranged them in the best possible order. But this allows that there might be a set of different but better parts arranged in the same order that would result in a better universe. And it also allows that each of the same parts might have been better (been higher up on the scale of perfection) so that when arranged in the same order the result is a better universe. In the first case we have an improvement by virtue of different but better parts in the same order. In the second case we have an improvement by virtue of the same parts being individually better but in the same order. Aquinas also allows that adding more parts may lead to a better world. For since there is an infinite distance between any creature and God, a world may be improved by adding more parts (species) between God and the highest presently existing creatures.

---

[5] A Particular Problem of Creation', 230.

[6] *Summa Theologica*, Ia. q. 25. a. 6. ad a. 3 (part I, question 25, article 6, reply to objection 3).

Reflecting on the above ways in which God could have made a better world, it seems that there simply is no end to increasingly better worlds that God could have created. For, to take just one type of case, given the infinite distance between the goodness of existing creatures and the goodness of God, and given that the value of a possible world reflects the value of the creatures who exist in that world, it seems to follow that there is an infinite number of increasingly better worlds. For, supposing that the highest creatures (creatures most like God) in a given world, W1, are human beings,[7] there would be a possible world, W2, with creatures that are one step higher (more nearly like God) than the world with humans. But then, surely, there would be a possible world, W3, with creatures that are one step higher (more nearly like God) than the creatures in W2, and so on ad infinitum. Now since the value of a well-ordered possible world reflects the value of its creatures, W1 is not as good a world as W2, W2 is not as good a world as W3, and so on ad infinitum. In short, there simply is no best world in the series. On this, or any similar scenario, whatever world God chooses to create, there would be a world he could have created instead whose inhabitants more closely approximate his absolute perfection. And if all this is so, there simply cannot be any such thing as a best possible world containing creatures. And this is just what Aquinas takes to be the truth of the matter. As Bruce Reichenbach explains,

It seems to be the case that when we speak of best as relating to the created world, we find that there is not a finite series such that there could be a best possible being or state of affairs. Rather we are faced with an infinite series of characteristics, degrees of their actualization, or optimific states of affairs, in which for any given being or state of affairs there will always be a better.[8]

One might object to Aquinas's view that there is an infinity of increasingly better worlds and, therefore, no best world by claiming that such a view cannot be true since each of these possible worlds includes God, an infinitely good, absolutely perfect being. And if each such world includes the infinite perfection of God, it would seem that no world can be better

---

[7] It won't matter if we include angels, and other possible denizens of the heavenly realm. For, since they too are created beings, there will be an infinite distance between them and God in terms of goodness.

[8] Bruce Reichenbach, 'Must God Create the Best Possible World?', *International Philosophical Quarterly,* 19 (1979), 208.

than another. For how could anything be better than a world that includes the infinite perfection of God? This objection, however, simply ignores Aquinas's view that a world, including its contents, is *created* by God and, therefore, cannot include God. So, if we think of a world simply in terms of the quality of its *parts* we cannot avoid the possibility that worlds with better parts are better worlds. And if there cannot be a *perfect, finite part*, then it seems that Aquinas and Reichenbach are right to conclude that there cannot be a best world. But this just takes us back to the question of how we should think of a world. Should we think of a world as constituted by its ordered parts *minus God*, or should God be included in our concept of a world?

I propose that we follow the road on which we began and continue thinking of a world, not as a whole consisting of created parts, but as a maximal state of affairs W such that for any state of affairs either it or its negation is included in W. On this account a world must either include God's existing or include God's not existing. And if we assume that God not only exists but *necessarily* exists, then every possible world must include God's existing.[9] If so, then to return to the objection noted above, how can we think that one world is better than another? For, assuming that God necessarily exists, every possible world includes an infinite amount of good by virtue of including the infinite goodness of God. How then can we say that one world is better than another when each contains an infinite amount of good? Could a world contain an amount of good that exceeds an infinite amount of good? And, in addition, one might well ask what sense it makes to speak of God's creating a world. For on the conception of a world as a maximal state of affairs, if God necessarily exists, then every world includes God's existing. But if God creates a world then aren't we implying that God creates himself, given that God's existing is a part of the world God creates?

Let's begin with the second question. Consider a world that includes both there being human beings and the number 4 being larger than the number 3. To create such a world God must do what is necessary to make it true that there are human beings and that the number 4 is larger than the number 2. But the number 4's being larger than the number 2 is a *necessary* state of affairs—it obtains in every possible world. Being

---

[9] Alternatively, if we think of God's existence as contingent, then among the possible worlds there will be bad worlds that include God's not existing. For no bad world could include God's existence if the creation of that world would require its creation by God.

necessary, it is already there, so to speak, a part of every possible world. So, if a possible world includes there being human beings and the number 4's being larger than the number 2, all God needs to do to be certain that a world he creates includes those two states of affairs is to create some human beings. In short, if a state of affairs is necessary, then by bringing about the non-necessary states of affairs making up a world God thereby brings about a world containing both those non-necessary states of affairs and the necessary state of affairs.[10] And, of course, this point applies also to God's necessarily existing, a state of affairs that is a constituent of every possible world.[11] In creating a world God *creates* (makes actual) the contingent states of affairs contained in that world.[12] In so doing there results a possible world containing those contingent states of affairs as well as states of affairs involving the nonexistence of contingent things God doesn't create—there being stones, there being human beings, there being no unicorns, etc.—and all the necessary states of affairs, including of course, God's existing. What if God is not a necessary being? If God is not a necessary being then, provided he exists, his creative activity accounts for the existence of all other contingent beings. And since, given the nature of God, no other being could account for his existence, God's existence would lack an explanation. Moreover, a world that includes God's being actual would also lack a *complete* explanation. For although the contingent states of affairs in that world, *other than God's existence*, would be due, directly or indirectly, to God's creative acts, God's own existence would be contingent and unexplained. Could not God's existence somehow be due to God even if he were contingent? No. If God is contingent rather than a necessarily existing being, then even if he always has existed and always will, God could not be the explanation for his own existence. Hence, there could be no complete explanation of why a given world containing God is in fact the actual world.

Let's turn now to our first question. Since any world that includes God's existence thereby contains an infinite amount of goodness, what

[10] This does not mean that there is *no way* in which necessary facts such as the number 4's being larger than the number 2 *depend* on God. It only means that God doesn't *create* them.

[11] God's necessarily existing is a constituent of every possible world provided God's necessarily existing is a possible state of affairs.

[12] Suppose God creates living creatures who in turn create some works of art. There being such works of art is a contingent state of affairs not directly created (made actual) by God. But these works of art would not exist had God not created living creatures. So, ultimately, all contingent states of affairs depend for their existence on God's creative activity.

sense can be made of saying of two worlds containing God that one is *better than* another? For it seems that we cannot have an amount of goodness that exceeds an infinite amount of goodness. And any world that includes an infinitely perfect being will include an infinite amount of goodness. To answer this question we need to distinguish the *qualitative* goodness of a world from its *quantitative* goodness. Putting God to one side for the moment, consider a world containing an *infinite* number of sentient beings each experiencing a certain degree of pleasure and no amount of pain. Their lives, we may suppose, are as happy as they can be given their limited needs and desires. How much good does the world contain? Well, given that pleasure itself is something that is intrinsically good, the world contains an infinite amount of good. For each sentient being experiences a finite amount of pleasure, and there is an infinite number of sentient creatures.[13] With its infinite number of sentient beings, each experiencing the satisfaction of eating food it desires, this world contains an infinite amount of pleasure or satisfaction. Consider now a different possible world in which there is an infinite number of higher-order sentient creatures experiencing not just the satisfaction of eating nourishing and pleasant-tasting food but also what are sometimes described as the higher-order pleasures of listening to fine music, viewing beautiful works of art, and participating in deep personal friendships and loving relationships. Suppose we agree that each of these two worlds contains an infinite *amount* of goodness. Would not the second world still be rightly judged to be a better world? If we say yes, as I think we should, it cannot be the *quantity* of good that makes the second world the better world. For each world, we suppose, contains an infinite amount of good. Rather, our judgment must be that although neither world contains a greater amount of good than the other, the world with the higher-order pleasures is *qualitatively* better than the world containing only the lower-order pleasures.

Is there a world than which no world is qualitatively better? We've seen that two worlds may contain an infinite amount of good, and yet one may be better than another by virtue of containing higher quality goods. For a world to be such that no world can be better than it there must be an *intrinsic maximum* to the qualitative goodness of a world. We

---

[13] If there is a difficulty in supposing an absolutely infinite number of lower-order sentient creatures exist at one time, we may think of the world as infinitely old and as always having such creatures in it. In this scenario there would not be a first lower-order sentient creature. Aquinas did not think that human reason could rule out the world as having always existed.

can see this by comparison with a being such that no being can be better than it (God). Consider the qualities of knowledge, power, and goodness that are central to the theistic idea of God. These are better-making qualities. A being who has them, it is thought, is better than a being who lacks them. But these qualities come in degrees. One being may have a greater degree of knowledge, power, or goodness than another. Other things being equal, a being that has a greater degree of any of the better-making qualities is superior to a being who possesses a lesser degree of that better-making quality. But what if there is no highest degree (intrinsic maximum) of one or more of these better-making qualities? In that case, since any being who has such a quality must have a certain degree of it, there could not be a best possible being. For given that there is no highest degree of that quality it would always be possible for there to be a being with a still greater degree of that quality. So, as the long tradition of theism in the West has recognized, if there is to be a best possible being, the better-making qualities must be such that there is a highest possible degree of each of them. And a similar point holds if there is to be a world than which no better world is possible. Therefore, if there is to be a best possible world, whatever qualities make for a better world must have intrinsic maxima, a degree beyond which no greater degree is possible. Otherwise, it is not possible for there to be a best possible world.

What then are the qualities that make for superior worlds? And are these qualities such that they have intrinsic maximums, a degree beyond which no greater degree is possible? Unlike determining the qualities that make for better persons, it is profoundly difficult to be confident in determining the qualities that make for better worlds. And more difficult still to determine that such qualities have intrinsic maximums, a degree beyond which no greater degree is possible. Of course, we would likely think that containing living things is a better-making quality with respect to possible worlds. After all, it is very doubtful that a lifeless world would contain much in the way of intrinsic value. But does the property of containing living things have an intrinsic maximum? As we've noted, Aquinas, unlike Leibniz, does not think there is a best world. But both emphasize the immense variety of living beings in the world as a sign of its degree of perfection. Perhaps, then, the value of a world consists not in the number of living things it contains but in the variety of such things. Indeed, Leibniz seems to have thought that God's purpose in creation was to realize the greatest variety of living things possible. He thought that each kind of living thing has a right to exist (i.e., to have existing members of that kind) and that the best arrangement of things would therefore be the one in which the greatest variety of living things is permitted to exist. Perhaps, then, the idea is that (1) there is an intrinsic maximum to the variety of living things that can exist and flourish, a degree of variety among living things than which there cannot be a greater degree of variety, and (2) that a world containing such a variety is a world than which there cannot be a better world. Of course, there cannot be a limit to the variety of kinds of living things unless there is an intrinsic maximum as we proceed up the ladder of kinds of living things. But that there is a best among kinds of living things is assured given that God is the best possible living thing.

In a remarkable book, *The Great Chain of Being*,[14] Arthur Lovejoy argued that such an idea has a long history in Western thought and enjoyed a profound influence on Augustine, Aquinas, Leibniz, and many other religious thinkers. He calls the idea 'the Principle of Plentitude', the principle 'that the extent and abundance of the creation must be as great as the possibility of existence and commensurate with the productive capacity of a "perfect" and inexhaustible Source . . .' (52). Finding its origin in Plato, Lovejoy notes the flourishing of this idea in Neoplatonism, and contends that its impact on medieval Christendom is largely due to Augustine and pseudo-Dionysius.[15] To understand the principle of plentitude, let's begin by asking why God would create any kinds of creatures other than the very best kind of creatures, those creatures that most closely resemble God. Why does God create the lower forms of living things, things devoid of reason and the capacity to worship God? The answer of the Neoplatonists, as we've noted, is that there is something intrinsically good in many different things being brought into existence regardless of their rank in the order of being and goodness. Lovejoy quotes Augustine as saying in response to the question of why God created lower as well as the highest creatures, 'if all things were equal, all things would not be; for the multiplicity of kinds of things of

---

[14] Arthur O. Lovejoy, *The Great Chain of Being* (1963; Cambridge, Mass.: Harvard University Press, 1978). Further page references to this edition will appear in the text.

[15] As we earlier noted, due in part to the mistake of attributing the writings of psuedo-Dionysius to the Dionysius mentioned in the Bible as associated with the Apostle Paul, the writings of this Neoplatonist were accorded great respect by medieval thinkers. And Aquinas was no exception. As a young man he was sent by his religious superiors to Paris where he transcribed the lectures of Albert on Dionysius. See Brian Davies, *The Thought of Thomas Aquinas* (Oxford: Clarendon Press, 1993), 4.

which the universe is constituted—first and second and so on, down to the creatures of the lowest grades—would not exist' (67). The implication of Augustine's remark is that it is intrinsically better that many *kinds* of beings exist, rather than just the best kind of beings. Moreover, it is the mark of a being of infinite love to extend love without regard to the rank of beings in the great chain of being.

One cannot help but suspect that the development of the idea that variety among kinds of beings is a great intrinsic good resulted from human beings looking around our world, with all its variety of animal life, and wondering what could possibly be the divine reason for it all. Nor can one avoid seeing in this idea an attempt to answer the question of why God would create beings of lesser value and ability than others. The answer developed by religious thinkers is that it is intrinsically valuable for there to be kinds of beings that are deficient (in comparison with superior kinds of being). Lovejoy cites Abelard (1079–1142) as follows:

It is not to be doubted that all things, both good and bad, proceed from a most perfectly ordered plan, that they occur and are fitted to one another in such a way that they could not possibly occur more fittingly. Thus Augustine: since God is good, evils would not be, unless it were a good that there should be evils. For by the same reason for which he wills that good things shall exist, namely, because their existence is befitting, he also wills that evil things should exist, . . . all of which as a whole tends to his greater glory. For as a picture is often more beautiful and worthy of commendation if some colors in themselves ugly are included in it, than it would be if it were uniform and of a single color, so from an admixture of evils the universe is rendered more beautiful and worthy of commendation. (72)[16]

The difficulty with the Neoplatonic idea that goodness is diffusive of itself is that it naturally leads to the *necessity* of God's creating a world composed of all kinds of beings, whatever their degree of perfection may be. For God's goodness is essential to him. He cannot not be other than supremely good and loving. And if good is necessarily diffusive of itself, then it appears that God cannot but create the fullest manifestation of goodness, the very best arrangement of all that is good. No medieval theologian saw this more clearly than Abelard. Lovejoy again quotes Abelard:

---

[16] *Epitome Theological Christianae*, in Migne, *Patr. Lat.*, vol. 178, col. 1726 (Lovejoy's trans.).

We must inquire whether it was possible for God to make more things or better things than he has in fact made. . . . Whether we grant this or deny it, we shall fall into many difficulties because of the apparent unsuitability of the conclusions to which either alternative leads us. For if we assume that he could make either more or fewer things than he has, we shall say what is exceedingly derogatory to his supreme goodness. Goodness, it is evident, can produce only what is good; but if there are things good which God fails to produce when he might have done so, or if he refrains from producing some things fit to be produced, who would not infer that he is jealous or unjust—especially since it costs him no labor to make anything? Hence is that most true argument of Plato's, whereby he proves that God could not in any wise have made a better world than he has made. (71)[17]

Against the background of God's manifesting his goodness being his aim in creating, Aquinas sought to avoid the necessitarian impulses contained in the Neoplatonic framework inherited by pseudo-Dionysius and suggested in the writings of Abelard.[18] Here is how Aquinas puts the problem that confronts him:

But, if the divine will of necessity wills the divine goodness and the divine being, it might seem to someone that it wills of necessity other things as well, since God wills all other things in willing His own goodness, . . . [19]

We can appreciate the difficulty Aquinas here faces without reviewing all his reasons for holding that God wills all other things in willing his own goodness. His main reason seems to be this. What we love for its own sake we want to be most perfect and to be multiplied as much as possible. And if we can't multiply what we love for its own sake, then we naturally wish to multiply what resembles it most. God, of course, loves his own nature for its own sake. But his nature cannot itself be multiplied. But what resembles God's nature most is the multitude of things, ideas of which are present in God's mind. So, God wills these things in virtue of willing himself. By some such line of reasoning as this Aquinas reaches the conclusion that God wills all other things in willing his own goodness. The problem he faces is avoiding the apparent implication that since God necessarily wills his own goodness he must also necessarily will the existence of all other things. He seeks to prove

---

[17] *Theologiae 'scholarium'*, 27–30 (Lovejoy's trans.).

[18] Kretzmann notes that Abelard was condemned at the Council of Sens for maintaining that God could not do otherwise than he does. See Kretzmann, 'A General Problem of Creation', n. 37.

[19] *Summa contra Gentiles*, lib. 1 d. 81 n. 1.

that this 'apparent implication' is in fact a false implication by pointing out that since God's goodness is infinite it can be participated in 'in infinite ways' and in ways other than by the creatures that now exist. I take him to imply by this that it is possible that other (kinds of) creatures should also exist now. But if God *necessarily* wills the existence of all other things, these other creatures would now exist, and plainly they do not. Since this line of argument is fairly crucial in his effort to avoid the necessity of the created world, it is worth our careful attention. Here is his argument in full.

Moreover, God, in willing His own goodness, wills things other than Himself to be in so far as they participate in His goodness. But, since the divine goodness is infinite, it can be participated in in infinite ways, and in ways other than it is participated in by the creatures that now exist. If, then, as a result of willing His own goodness, God necessarily willed the things that participate in it, it would follow that He would will the existence of an infinity of creatures participating in His goodness in an infinity of ways. This is patently false, because, if He willed them, they would be, since His will is the principle of being for things, . . . Therefore God does not necessarily will even the things that now exist.[20]

Aquinas is quite explicit in saying that in necessarily willing his own goodness God *thereby* wills other things than himself to exist. He wills them to be by virtue of the fact that they participate in his goodness. It would seem to follow from this that the existence of those possible things is necessary. Against this conclusion he gives an *empirical* argument, pointing out that many possible things do not in fact exist. Since these possible beings do not in fact exist, it cannot follow from the necessary existence of God that their existence is necessary. For example, it is reasonable to think that between humans and angels there are possible beings God could have added to his creation. These intermediate creatures, were they to have been created, would have manifested God's goodness. But since no such intermediate creatures exist, it follows that God does not *necessarily* will the existence of things that manifest his goodness.

For this argument to be successful two assumptions implied by Aquinas's reasoning must be true. First, it must be possible for there to exist creatures of kinds that in fact don't exist in our world. Second, it must be true that the world would have been *better* (a better world would have been actual) if there were creatures of more kinds in existence than there in fact are. For unless this second assumption is true, it could be

---

[20] Ibid., n. 4.

that our world—even given that it lacks instances of kinds of creatures that God could have created—is the best world (or as good a world as) God could create. And if that could be so, then even though God necessarily wills the existence of things that participate in his goodness, God's overall desire to create the best world would outweigh his effectively willing the existence of more things (or kinds of things) that participate in his goodness. That is, his necessarily willing the existence of things that participate in his goodness would have the same status as his necessarily willing that all human beings be saved—it would express God's antecedent will, but not his all things considered will. For if there is a best world that God can create, his all things considered will would be to create that world.

Even if we put to one side the question of whether there is a best world among the worlds God can create, there are two problems with Aquinas's argument. First, how does he know that there are kinds of beings that don't exist in the actual world? Aquinas thinks the answer is obvious. And it does seem that we can imagine beings that God could have created but did not—for example, beings between humans and angels. But how do we *know* that God hasn't created beings between humans and angels? We know, says Aquinas, because 'If he willed them, they would be.' I take him to mean that these beings would exist *now*. And the problem here is that for beings of certain kinds to necessarily exist in a world it is not required that they exist at *all times* in that world. If something necessarily exists at some time or other, but not at all times, it necessarily exists in the world. But none of us is in a position to survey the entire universe (all that exists now, did exist, or will exist in the future). At most we can make some judgments about what things exist when we are around to take note of them. But we are hardly in a position to determine with any certainty what kinds of things existed in the past, will exist in the future, or exist now but in regions of the universe beyond our capacity to discern. For us to be sure that there are kinds of things that have no instances in our universe we must suppose that if things of a certain kind do exist then instances of them exist at every time in the universe and at every place in the universe. But this assumption lacks justification.

Second, there is a modal difficulty in Aquinas's argument. Consider the hypothetical proposition: If God wills his own goodness then he wills the existence of things other than himself. Why does Aquinas think this if-then proposition is true? It is because, as he tells us, God's love of his own goodness implies a desire to multiply it, a desire that can be satisfied only by multiplying what most resembles his nature: things other than himself. So, given that God's own nature necessarily cannot be multiplied, and given that his love for his nature is, therefore, necessarily directed to multiplying what resembles most his nature—things other than himself—God necessarily creates a world of things.[21]

Let's now ask what Aquinas must say in response to the following question: Is there a possible world in which God wills his own goodness but does not will the existence of things other than himself? Recall what Aquinas says: 'God wills all other things in willing His own goodness.' Does Aquinas mean to imply that God does this in some possible worlds but not in others? Does he mean to imply that in some possible world God wills and loves his own essence but does not will the multitude of things? If he meant that then he could hardly say that 'God wills the multitude of things *in willing and loving* His own essence and perfection.' Consider again the reasoning he gives in support of the proposition that God wills all other things in willing his own nature.

1. God's love of his nature for its own sake is absolutely necessary.
2. What God loves for its own sake he wants to be multiplied as much as possible.
3. God cannot multiply his own nature.
4. If God cannot multiply what God loves for its own sake then he wills to multiply what is most like what he loves for its own sake.
5. Since all other things participate in God's goodness they are most like what he loves for its own sake.

From these principles Aquinas concludes that

6. God wills all other things in willing his own nature.

The only premiss in this argument whose necessity is open to question is (4). And it is reasonably clear, I believe, that it is the premiss whose purported necessity Aquinas means to challenge. The problem for Aquinas is to justify holding that God's willing the multitude of things is a contingent fact given that he takes it to be implied by, if not included in, what is clearly for him a necessary fact: God's willing and loving himself. As he says: 'God, therefore, wills the multitude of things in willing and loving His own essence and perfection.'[22] Clearly, the natural

---

[21] For Aquinas, God's love for his nature (his goodness) is also a necessary feature of God. There is no possible world in which God fails to love his own nature.

[22] Ibid., lib. 1, d. 75 n. 3.

reading of this claim is that *God's wills and loves his own essence and perfection* logically implies *God's wills the multitude of things*. But if p logically implies q, and p is necessary, q must be necessary as well. So, either Aquinas must admit that God necessarily wills the multitude of things or he must reject either that God necessarily wills and loves his own essence and perfection or that God wills the multitude of things in willing and loving his own essence and perfection.

It would be a mistake to claim that there is a demonstrable contradiction in Aquinas's view that God was free not to create a world. In fact, he endeavors to avoid contradiction by trying to distinguish two ways in which one can will X in willing Y. If Y can exist without X then Aquinas thinks that although one wills X in willing Y, one need not necessarily will X if one must necessarily will Y. And since he clearly thinks God can exist without other things existing, he thinks he is free to hold that God's willing X is contingent, whereas his willing Y is necessary. In some such way as this he endeavors to hold that even though in willing his existence he thereby wills the existence of other things, and he necessarily wills his own existence, he does not necessarily will the existence of other things. But it is fair to say that there is a serious tension in his thinking about God's freedom with respect to creation, a tension due to his effort to reconcile God's freedom not to create with the Dionysian line that 'the good is diffusive of itself and of being'. And we've noted that Norman Kretzmann, a prominent philosopher and major scholar on the thought of Aquinas, thinks that the Dionysian line is so strongly supported by Aquinas that he (Aquinas) should have concluded that God is not free not to create. But we must now return to our central concern in this chapter: Aquinas's reasons for denying that there is a best possible world.

As we've learned, Aquinas takes a world to consist of parts (various kinds of things) in a certain order. And he holds that given the parts in the world, God could not have ordered them better than he has. So, in one respect the world could not be better than it is—given its parts they could not have been placed in a better order. But there are ways in which God could have created a better world. Let's focus our attention on just one of these ways: the addition of more parts. A world must contain a certain number of parts. But since there is an infinite distance between any part and God, a world can always be improved by adding more parts (species) between God and the highest presently existing parts (species). And since the addition of better parts to the presently existing world would seem to result in a greater quantity of good in the world, it does seem that there cannot be a best world. For any finite world (*a*) has a definite number of parts, and (*b*) is such that between its best parts and God there could always be added better and better finite parts. It seems, then, that there is no such thing as Leibniz's best possible world. For whatever world God creates, it will be true that God could have created a better world. And this is the conclusion Kretzmann comes to in his careful study of Aquinas on creation. He concludes 'that perfectly good (omniscient, omnipotent) God must create a world less good (in respect of the richness of its sets of parts, for example) than one he could create.'[23]

Earlier we came to the conclusion that if two worlds contain an infinitely perfect being (God) it is a mistake to think that one of them can be *quantitatively better* than another. It is a mistake because each world contains an infinite amount of good in the person of God. So, the mere fact (should it be a fact) that one world containing God has a greater amount of good among finite sentient creatures than the other world containing God will not make it a quantitatively better world than the other. For by virtue of containing God both will still contain an infinite amount of good. But the fact that one world is not quantitatively better than another does not mean that it is not a better world than another. For one of the worlds still may be qualitatively better than the other by virtue of containing an infinite amount of higher-order good, as compared to the infinite amount of lesser-order good contained by the other world. And my suggestion is that once we allow that God (an infinitely good being) is included in every possible world we should then rank worlds not in terms of the quantity of good they contain but in terms of the quality of good they contain. I make this suggestion not to undermine the anti-Leibnizian claim that there is no best world, but, in part, to protect it from an objection based on the fact that since there cannot be a greater quantity of good than is represented by the infinite goodness of God, every world containing God is equally good. For once that objection is accepted the search will be on to rank worlds by some other means than their respective quantity of good, leaving open the possibility that there is a best world. And my suggestion is that two worlds can contain the same quantity of good, and yet one be qualitatively better than another. A world with an infinite number of happy pigs

---

[23] 'A Particular Problem of Creation', 238. Kretzmann says 'must create' because he departs from Aquinas in holding that God is not free not to create some world or other.

has an infinite quantity of good in it, as does a world with an infinite number of human beings enjoying great happiness. But the second world will be rightly judged—at least by non-pigs—to be a better world. Of course, one may object that since God is a necessary being, he is a constituent of every world. And since the goodness of God is both quantitatively and qualitatively infinite, the world with an infinite number of happy pigs will be not just quantitatively as good, but qualitatively as good as the world with an infinite number of human beings enjoying great happiness. This point, however, rests on the questionable assumption that the qualitative goodness of a world may just be a function of the qualitative goodness of one or more of the constituent beings in that world. And it is this assumption that seems to be precluded in the idea that (other things being equal) a world with a greater *variety of living things* is a better world. For it is this idea that Augustine, Aquinas, and Leibniz used to explain why our world contains the enormous variety of living things, other than God and humans. So, a world containing only God and the angels, say, is simply not as good as a world containing God, angels, humans, and all the creatures that make up our world. And this means that the qualitative goodness of a world isn't a function of the qualitative goodness of the best being in that world, even if that being is infinitely good.

Where does all this leave us? We've concluded that of two worlds containing (God), neither can be quantitatively better than the other, but one may be qualitatively better than another. A world with God and a variety of creatures, including humans, who have lives that are both good and happy is a qualitatively better world than a world containing God and a variety of creatures, including humans, who have lives that are either not good or not happy. So, even though God's goodness is quantitatively and qualitatively infinite, one world containing God may be a qualitatively better world than another containing God, owing to its creatures having qualitatively better lives. And this leaves open the possibility that there may be a best among possible worlds. So, it is perhaps a mistake to think that Aquinas has established that there is no best possible world. On the other hand, I certainly do not think we can prove that there is a best world among possible worlds. Nor do I think we can prove that there is a world so good that no world is better than it, although some other worlds may be as good as it. And, therefore, what I propose to examine in succeeding chapters is the question whether God can enjoy any significant degree of freedom with respect to creating a world if (1) there is a best world, (2) there are several equally good worlds and none better, or (3) for any world there is a better world. Concerning (1) we have already reached the preliminary conclusion that God is not free with respect to creation, that his absolute perfections provide him no choice other than creating the best world. Indeed, he creates it of necessity, not freely. Our preliminary conclusion concerning (2) is that God would then enjoy freedom to choose among the equally good worlds, but his choice among them would have to be based on considerations other than the degree of good that the world possesses. In a later chapter we will consider the implications for God's existence and freedom given the supposition that (3) for any world there is a better world.

4

Jonathan Edwards on Divine and Human Freedom

A book on the topic of divine freedom must come to grips with the penetrating discussion of freedom, both human and divine, by Jonathan Edwards[1] (1703–58), the greatest American philosophical theologian of the eighteenth century. In his day there was a struggle between two theological traditions: Calvinism and Arminianism. Calvinism, a movement originating with the work of John Calvin (1509–64), endeavored to reconcile our longings for freedom of the will with both the philosophical view of universal causation and the theological view of divine predestination. Arminianism, a view originating with the Dutch theologian Jacobus Arminius (1560–1609), advocated a stronger conception of human freedom than Calvinism allowed, a conception according to which a free agent has a power of willing and doing otherwise than he in fact does. Consequently, Arminianism denied universal causation and total divine predestination. It seemed clear to the Arminians, for example, that if some action of ours was causally necessitated by an unbroken chain of causes proceeding from the distant past, then at the time we performed that action it was not really *up to us* whether we would do that action or refrain from doing it. For, given universal causation, the occurrence of that action was the inevitable result of a

---

[1] Jonathan Edwards, *Freedom of the Will*, ed. Paul Ramsey (New Haven: Yale University Press, 1957). Unless otherwise stated, when this work is quoted or there is a reference to Edward's *Freedom of the Will* the expression in parentheses following the quotation refers to the part and section of this work, e.g. I. 3 refers to pt I, sect. 3.

series of causes stretching into the distant past. So, if it were up to us whether to perform or not perform that action it must have been up to us to determine what happened in the distant past. The past, however, seems to be totally beyond our control. We may regret certain things we did in the past. But it is not in our power to alter the past. As Aristotle observed:

No one deliberates about the past but only about what is future and capable of being otherwise, while what is past is not capable of not having taken place; hence Agathon is right in saying: 'For this alone is lacking, even in God, to make undone things that have once been done.'[2]

Perhaps we can see the attractiveness of the Arminian view of freedom if we contrast our view of the past with a common assumption about the future. Unlike the past, we commonly think the future is open, that it is now up to us to determine which of several different possible paths into the future we shall take. Although we know that only one of these possible paths into the future will be followed, we believe that it is sometimes up to us *which possible path* into the future we shall take. For example, a college graduate may have an opportunity to take a position with General Motors or to go on to law school instead. Moreover, that college graduate may well believe that it is now up to her which of these two possibilities she will pursue—up to her, therefore, whether the near future will find her at General Motors or, instead, in law school. We think, then, that sometimes we have an important kind of control over the future, limited as that control may be. Such control consists in *freedom to do otherwise*, the power we possess to make any one of two or more alternative paths into the future the path we shall actually follow. Moreover, we believe that the possession of such power is required if we are to be genuinely responsible for the particular path we take into the future.

As the Arminian about free will sees it, there are two threats to the idea that we possess any control at all over what path we shall take into the future. One threat is posed by causal determinism, the view that the past and the laws of nature logically determine the particular path into the future we shall follow. The other threat is posed by the existence of an essentially omniscient, eternal being whose past decisions or beliefs regarding our future conduct logically imply which particular path into

---

[2] Aristotle, *Nicomachean Ethics*, VII, 2. 1139b, in *The Basic Works of Aristotle*, ed. Richard McKeon (New York: Random House, 1941).

the future we shall follow. The importance of Edwards lies in his brilliant effort to do two things: (1) to reconcile human freedom and moral responsibility with causal determinism and divine predestination,[3] and (2) to attack the understanding of freedom and responsibility advocated by the Arminians.

I

Edwards begins his treatise on Freedom of the Will by posing the question: What is the Will? His answer is that the will is the power of the mind to choose. An act of will, therefore, is simply the mind's choosing (willing) some action or some course of action. The object of a volition (an act of will) is, according to Edwards, always an action. It is important to note that 'action' is used very broadly by Edwards to refer both to doing something (e.g., drinking a glass of wine that has been offered) and to not doing something (e.g., not drinking a glass of wine that has been offered). What, then, determines which action (drinking the wine, not drinking the wine) the agent performs? Edwards argues that the agent performs that action which 'appears most agreeable to the agent'. Now, it may be that refraining from drinking *is* what is most agreeable, at least in the long run. But what determines the action performed is what *appears* to be most agreeable to the agent. Indeed, Edwards thinks that even if the man reasons that he would be better off in the long run by not taking the drink, he still may take the drink owing to 'taking the drink' *appearing* to be most agreeable to the man.

Edwards adopts what he thinks is the ordinary notion of 'liberty' (freedom): that we are free if we are able to do as we please (I. 5). We may take Edwards to be here saying that we are free with respect to a certain action A just in case we can do A if we so will (choose) and can refrain from doing A if we will (choose) to refrain. An important point about this conception of freedom is that it does not imply anything about how the agent comes by his act of will. 'Let the person come by his volition or choice how he will, yet, if he is able, and there is nothing in the way to hinder his pursuing and executing his will, the man is fully and perfectly free, according to the primary and common notion of freedom' (I. 5). Moreover, Edwards's conception of a free act does not

---

[3] Our main concern will be with the threat of causal determinism to human freedom.

even imply that the agent *could* have refrained from willing the act. All it implies is that *if* the agent were to will to refrain, he would have the power to carry out that act of will—i.e., the power to refrain from performing that action. It is this last point that separates the Arminian conception of freedom from Edwards's conception. If the person is *unable to will* to refrain from doing A then, according to the Arminians, refraining from doing A is *not* in that person's power, whether or not the man has the capacity to carry out the choice to refrain, should that choice somehow occur. Edwards's position is clear: '... a man can't be truly said to be unable to do a thing, when he can do it *if* he will' (I. 4; emphasis mine). The point here is this: there might not be anything that would prevent someone from doing a certain thing *if* he should choose to do it, and yet it might be true that there is something that prevents that person from *choosing* to do that thing. For Edwards all that matters, so far as freedom is concerned, is that the person would have been able to do that thing *if* he had willed (chosen) to do it. The issue of whether he could have willed to do it has no real bearing on the question of whether he was *free* to perform that action. For the Arminians, however, it must be true that the person *could* have willed to do (not to do) that act, if it is to be true that the person was free to do (not to do) that act.

It is difficult to overemphasize the importance of this difference between Edwards and the Arminians. Let us suppose that someone is so addicted to alcohol that in certain circumstances when a cup of alcohol is offered to him he is simply incapable of choosing to reject the cup. Indeed, let us say that his addiction is so strong that in these circumstances he simply *cannot* refrain from accepting the drink and consuming it. In short, it is not in his power to refrain from accepting and consuming the drink. Of course, it isn't true that he lacks the *physical power* to reject the drink. It is not as though someone overpowers him and forces his fingers to take hold of the cup, forces his arm to move so that the cup is brought to his mouth, etc. He doesn't lack power over the movement of his fingers and limbs. What he lacks is power over his will. He is simply unable to refrain from *choosing* to drink the alcohol. Here we may distinguish between his physical power and his mental or psychological power. He certainly has the physical power to refrain from accepting and consuming the drink. What he lacks is power over his will. He cannot bring himself to refrain from willing (choosing) to accept the cup and drink the alcohol. If all this is so, how are we to understand Edwards's claim?

It can't truly be said, according to ordinary use of language, that . . . a drunkard, let his appetite be never so strong, can't keep the cup from his mouth. (I. 4)

We must understand Edwards to be saying that 'according to ordinary use of language' the question of whether a drunkard can or cannot keep the cup from his mouth is to be decided solely on the grounds of whether the drunkard has the *physical power* to bring the cup to his mouth, as well as the *physical power* not to bring it to his mouth. And so long as the drunkard is in command of his limbs it will be a mistake, according to Edwards, to say that he *can't* keep the cup from his mouth. And this will be so even though the drunkard is *incapable* of choosing to keep the cup from his mouth.

I suppose there is a fact of the matter as to whether Edwards is or is not correct when he says: 'It can't truly be said, according to ordinary use of language, that . . . a drunkard, let his appetite be never so strong, can't keep the cup from his mouth.' Perhaps when he wrote these words in the eighteenth century the ordinary use of language at the time was such that no matter how *addicted* a drunkard might be it would not be a correct use of language to then say 'He can't keep the cup from his mouth.' For concerning the actions we perform by moving our hands and limbs, it is sufficient for Edwards to conclude that the drunkard can keep the cup from his mouth provided that he can so move his hands *if* he wills to do so. And, of course, given his addiction, it may be true both that while holding the cup the drunkard can move his hands away from his mouth *if* he wills to do so and that he *cannot* will to so move his hands and limbs. The fact that the person cannot will to keep the cup from his mouth doesn't preclude it being true that the person can keep the cup from his mouth *if* he were to will to do so. The fact that one is unable to will to do a certain thing doesn't imply that the person would be unable to do that thing if he were to will to do it.

Edwards distinguishes two sorts of inability that preclude us from voluntarily performing various actions. A human being is unable to fly by simply flapping his arms. And this is so even if he should somehow choose (will) to fly by flapping his arms. He cannot perform the willed action because, as Edwards would say, 'nature won't allow it'. Nature has endowed birds with the ability to fly by flapping their wings. But nature has not endowed humans with the ability to fly by flapping their arms. As Edwards notes: 'We are said to be *naturally* unable to do a thing, when we can't do it if we will' (I. 4). The reason why we can't do it even if we should will to do it is either because nature hasn't equipped us to do it or because of some obstacle external to our will that prevents us from doing it, an obstacle that we are unable to remove. In addition to *natural inability* to engage in a certain action, an inability that presupposes factors external to the will which prevent the person from so acting if he should will so to act, there is also, as Edwards is careful to note, *moral inability*. Moral inability is present whenever factors such as habits, dispositions, and motives render us *unable to will* a certain act. Unlike natural inability, which applies to actions, moral inability applies not to actions but to volitions. Such inability consists in the inability to will to do a certain thing due either to a lack of motive to do that thing or the presence of strong contrary motives. Edwards gives several examples of moral inability.

A child of great love and duty to his parents, may be unable to be willing to kill his father. A drunkard, under such and such circumstances, may be unable to forbear taking of strong drink. A very malicious man may be unable to exert benevolent acts to an enemy, or to desire his prosperity: yea, some may be so under the power of vile disposition, that they may be unable to love those who are most worthy of their esteem and affection. A strong habit of virtue and great degree of holiness may cause a moral inability to love wickedness in general, may render a man unable to take complacence in wicked persons or things; or to choose a wicked life, and prefer it to a virtuous life. (I. 4)

Moral inability consists in the inability to will to do a certain act, as well the inability to will to refrain from doing a certain act. The moral saint may be unable to will to accept a bribe; whereas the moral sinner may be unable to will not to accept a bribe.

What we've just seen is that Edwards, no less than his Arminian opponents, is aware that there are two distinct questions that can be raised about human power or ability.

    I. Does the person have the power to do (to not do) the action in question should he will to do (will not to do) that action?

    II. Does the person have the power to will to do (will not to do) that action?

Question I concerns the agent's *natural* ability: it asks whether doing X (not doing X) is in the agent's power should he will to do (will not to do) X. Question II concerns the agent's *moral* ability: it asks whether willing to do X (willing not to do X) is in the agent's power. What separates Edwards from the Arminians is his view that *moral inability* has no bearing on the question of whether the agent is to be morally praised or blamed for doing (not doing) what he wills. So, if someone has a psychologically overpowering need to *will* to do something he has the power to do—and does it as a result of willing to do it—he not only does that thing *freely* on Edwards's account, he is, as well, *morally responsible* for doing it. And this is so even though he was *unable* to refrain from willing (choosing) to do it. The important point for Edwards is that the moral inability to refrain from willing to do what he did does not imply a natural inability (or lack of power) to refrain from doing that act. For the drunkard possesses the natural ability to refrain from picking up the drink and consuming it so long as it is true that *were he to will* not to take the drink he would be physically able *not* to pick up the drink and consume it. And the answer to this question will be 'Yes' so long as the agent has control over his limbs and fingers. Thus, as we've noted, Edwards claims: 'It can't truly be said, according to ordinary use of language, that ... a drunkard, let his appetite be never so strong, can't keep the cup from his mouth' (I. 4). For although the drunkard may be unable to prevent himself from *willing* to drink, it is true, nevertheless, that he has the physical power to refrain from drinking. He has the physical power to refrain from drinking simply because it is true that should he (somehow manage to) will to refrain from drinking he would have the physical ability to do so. And it does not matter that the drunkard is unable to will to refrain from drinking. Thus, for Edwards, the moral inability of the drunkard to will (choose) not to pick up the drink in no way excuses the drunkard from moral responsibility for picking up the drink. And the justification Edwards gives for holding that moral inability to refrain from choosing to pick up the drink doesn't excuse the drunkard for willing to pick up the drink and doing so is that, as Edwards sees it, in the ordinary use of language we do not refrain from morally evaluating humans for what they do as a result of choosing to do it. We hold the saint to be morally praiseworthy for not accepting the bribe, and it does not matter that he is unable to choose to accept the bribe. And we hold the sinner to be morally at fault for accepting the bribe, and it does not matter that he is unable to refrain from choosing to accept the bribe.

Before criticizing Edward's view that moral inability (being unable to refrain from choosing as one does) does not preclude an agent from moral praise or blame for what that agent chooses to do and does, it will be helpful to see the implications of Edwards's view on this matter for the question that is central to our investigation: Is an essentially perfect being to be morally praised and thanked for his always doing the best thing that he can? We have argued that it makes sense to morally praise and be thankful to a being who does what is best only if it is *possible* for that being to do otherwise. And, as we've observed, an essentially perfect being must of necessity do whatever it sees to be the best thing (all things considered) it can do. But this means, as Edwards is careful to note, that God necessarily chooses (wills) to do the best possible action (all things considered) for him to do. In short, given his necessary perfections, God is *morally unable* to do anything other than what he sees to be best. God is morally unable to do otherwise because although God is able to do otherwise *if* he chooses to, he cannot choose to do other than the best. But just as the drunkard (no matter how extreme his addiction) is not morally excused (from praise or blame) for taking the drink, so God, according to Edwards, is not morally excused (from praise or blame) for doing what he sees to be best. The drunkard is not excused from moral praise or blame because, according to the ordinary usage of language, a person who has it in his power not to pick up the cup of alcohol *should he will to do so*, is subject to moral praise or blame if he willfully picks up the cup and drinks from it. And the same usage of language dictates, Edwards believes, that a being who has the power not to do what is best, *should he will not to do what is best*, is subject to moral praise or blame if he willfully does what is best. To hold otherwise in either case, Edwards would say, is to misuse language. Indeed, Edwards argues rather effectively that Arminian theologians *praise* God for doing what is best while at the same time acknowledging that given his necessary perfections God is unable not to do what he sees to be best. Thus Edwards is able to point out an apparent inconsistency in the Arminian position. So far as human freedom is concerned, the Arminians argue that the *moral saint*, who cannot refrain from willing to do what is best, is not deserving of moral praise for willing and doing what is best. Whereas, with respect to God they argue that his *necessarily willing* to do what is best doesn't imply that he is not deserving of moral praise for willing and doing what is best.

In his dispute with some of the Arminian theologians of his day, it must be admitted, I believe, that Edwards is victorious in showing that God necessarily wills to do what he sees to be best. And since the Arminians hold that necessity in willing and acting precludes freedom in willing and acting, as well as moral praise or blame for so willing and acting, Edwards is successful in showing the Arminians to be simply inconsistent when it comes to thanking and praising God for doing what it was impossible for God to avoid doing. Of the three of his Arminian contemporaries (Thomas Chubb, Daniel Whitby, and Isaac Watts) that Edwards discusses with some care, it is Chubb and Watts who bear the brunt of his attack on the topic of divine freedom. For since the Arminians insist that power to will and do otherwise is essential to *freely* willing and doing, and also insist that *freely* willing and doing is essential to moral praise or blame for what one wills and does as a result of so willing, it is relatively easy to see the difficulty in praising God for willing and doing what he sees to be the best possible thing for him to do. And Edwards shows little mercy in driving this point home against Watts and his fellow Arminians. Indeed, with some flair he quotes at length from none other than the well-respected libertarian theologian Samuel Clarke, in showing that God possesses no Arminian liberty in willing to do what he sees to be best. Edwards quotes Clarke's recognition of the *moral necessity* of God's always choosing to do what he sees to be best:

Though God is a most perfectly free agent, yet he cannot but do always what is best in the whole. The reason is evident; because perfect wisdom and goodness are as steady and certain principles of action, as necessity itself; and an infinitely wise and good being, indued with the most perfect liberty, can no more choose to act in contradiction to wisdom and goodness, than a necessary agent can act contrary to the necessity by which it is acted; it being as great an absurdity and impossibility in choice, for infinite wisdom to choose to act unwisely, or infinite goodness to choose what is not good, as it would be in nature, for absolute necessity to fail of producing its necessary effect.[4]

Isaac Watts does seem to be aware of the threat to libertarian free will in the idea that an agent is necessarily determined to will and act according to the necessary determination of the understanding that a particular act is all things considered the best action for the agent to perform.

Edwards quotes Watts as follows:

The Scheme which determines the will always and certainly by the understanding, and the understanding by the appearance of things, seems to take away the true nature of vice and virtue. For the sublimest of virtues, and the vilest of vices, seem rather to be matters of fate and necessity, flowing naturally and necessarily

---

[4] *Freedom of the Will* (IV. 7). Edwards quotes from Clarke's *Demonstration of the Being and Attributes of God* (6th edn. London, 1725), 64.

from the existence, the circumstances, and present situation of persons and things: for this existence and situation necessarily makes such an appearance to the mind; from this appearance flows a necessary perception and judgment, concerning these things; this judgment necessarily determines the will: and thus by this chain of necessary causes, virtue and vice would lose their nature, and become natural ideas, and necessary things, instead of moral and free actions.[5]

But, as Edwards is then quick to point out, Watts also says: 'I grant, and always have granted, that wheresoever there is such an antecedent superior fitness of things, God acts according to it, so as never to contradict it; and particularly, in all his judicial proceedings, as a governor, and a distributer of rewards and punishments.'[6] Edwards also notes that Watts says: 'That it is not possible for God to act otherwise, than according to this fitness and goodness in things.'[7] Here then is Edwards's final judgment on Watts's reasoning:

. . . according to this author, putting these several passages of his *Essay* together, there is *no virtue, nor anything of a moral nature*, in the most sublime and glorious acts and exercises of God's holiness, justice, and faithfulness; and he never does anything which is in itself supremely worthy, and above all other things fit and excellent, but only as a kind of mechanical medium of fate; and in what he does as the judge, and *moral governor* of the world, he exercises no moral excellency; exercising no freedom in these things, because he acts by necessity; and therefore he only acts by an Hobbistical fatality; as 'a being indeed of vast understanding, as well as power and efficiency (as he said before) but without a will to choose, being a kind of almighty minister of fate, acting under its supreme influence.' For he allows, that in all these things God's will is determined constantly and certainly by a superior fitness, and that it is not possible for him to act otherwise. And if these things are so, what glory or praise belongs to God for doing holily and justly, or taking the most fit, holy, wise and excellent course, in any one instance? Whereas, according to the Scriptures, and also the common sense of mankind, it don't in the least derogate from the honor of any being, that through the moral perfection of his nature, he necessarily acts with supreme wisdom and holiness: but on the contrary, his praise is the greater wherein consists the height of his glory. (IV. 7)

Clearly, Edwards is on to an *inconsistency* in the Arminian treatment of freedom and responsibility. With respect to human behavior they count both natural and moral necessity as limitations on freedom. And this

---

[5] *Freedom of the Will* (IV. 7). The quoted passage is from Watts, *Essay on the Freedom of Will in God and Creatures* (1732).

[6] Ibid.

[7] Ibid.

seems exactly right so long as it is *libertarian freedom* that is at stake. For on the libertarian account of free action, an agent is free in willing and acting only if it was in the power of the agent not to have so willed and acted.[8] And an agent is free in refraining from willing and acting only if it was in the agent's power not to have so refrained from willing and acting. The compatibilist account of freedom, on the other hand, emphasizes freedom with respect to action but makes no demands on freedom with respect to willing, allowing that the agent may be free and responsible in performing an action even though, at the time of performing that action, it was not in the agent's power not to have so willed and acted. Of course, the compatibilist does allow that some factors depriving the agent of 'power not to have performed the action' are incompatible with the agent performing that action freely and being responsible for so acting. And those factors are roughly what Edwards delineates as rendering the agent *physically unable* to perform (to refrain from performing) the action in question should the agent will to perform (will to refrain from performing) that action. But factors rendering the agent *morally unable* to will to perform (to will to refrain from performing) the action in question do not, on Edwards's compatibilist account of freedom, render the agent unfree, nor do they deprive the agent of moral responsibility for his action. So the drunkard who is physically able to refrain from picking up the glass *should he will to do so*, is morally responsible for his act of picking it up and drinking from it, and it matters not at all that due to his addiction he is simply *unable* to refrain from willing (choosing) to pick up the glass and drink from it. For this is a moral inability, not a physical or natural inability.

It should be clear that the Arminian theologians cannot have it both ways. As proponents of libertarian freedom as *essential* for moral responsibility, they can't insist that *power not to will as one does* is required for a willed act to be free and, therefore, one for which an agent may be morally responsible, and then proceed to declare that God is not just free, but *perfectly free*, when he wills *of necessity* to always and unfailingly do what he sees is the best to be done. For then God is a necessary agent,

---

[8] As we've earlier noted, this is a simplification of the libertarian view. For first, on the libertarian agent-cause view, the agent is free in causing his volition (and the action flowing from that volition) provided the agent had the power not to cause his volition. And second, we need to note that an agent may be *derivatively responsible* for his volition and action even though he cannot avoid so willing and acting, provided he freely and intentionally brought about in himself the conditions that render his so willing and acting inevitable.

not a free agent. He lacks power over his will in that he is unable to will to refrain from doing what he sees is the best to be done. And it doesn't help much to say that in such cases he is not just free, but *perfectly* free. For, as we noted earlier in examining Clarke's appeal to God's 'perfect freedom' in *necessarily* always willing and doing what is best, Clarke simply forgets that he has all along insisted that freedom is a *two-way power*, involving both the power to will and act and the power not to so will and act. On Clarke's account of the nature of freedom, the power to choose otherwise is *necessary* for a choice to be free. Therefore, if it is not in God's power to choose to do evil, God does not freely choose not to do evil. And if it is not in God's power to choose to act contrary to what is best, God does not freely choose to do what is best. To call God's *necessary choice* to do what is best 'perfect freedom' is a colossal misuse of language. For it amounts to saying what is a necessary choice, and therefore, an unfree choice on God's part is, nevertheless, the very best example of a free and morally responsible choice.

II

Despite the force of the reasons Edwards advances in support of his view that moral inability, the inability not to will as one did (or the inability to will as one should), is *irrelevant* to the agent's moral responsibility for acting as he did (or for failing to act as one should), there are, I believe, sufficient grounds for rejecting Edwards's position on this matter. To begin, consider the case of Andrea Yates, a mentally ill woman who in June 2001 drowned her five children in a bathtub. With a long history of mental illness, including hospitalization, shock treatment, and considerable medication, Andrea, so the defense argued, was insane at the time she killed her five children and, therefore, innocent by reason of insanity. It was generally accepted that she had often needed treatment and displayed many signs of illness, including hallucinations, delusions, etc. If the jury found her to be legally insane, a hearing would be held to determine whether she would be released or involuntarily committed. The prosecution, however, argued that Andrea Yates was sane when she killed her children and they, therefore, were seeking the death penalty. If the jury found her to be legally sane and, therefore, guilty, they would then have to determine whether there is enough mitigating evidence to sentence her to life in prison rather than death. As it turned out, the jury did not find her to be insane at the time she killed her five children. But they voted that she be imprisoned for life rather than put to death.

What is of special interest here is what one must be able to demonstrate in court if one is to establish that Andrea Yates was insane at the time she drowned her children. According to Texas law, the defense had the burden of proving not only that Andrea suffered from a severe mental disease but also that she didn't know the difference between right and wrong at the time of the drownings. Although there was general agreement that Andrea had a history of mental illness, it was difficult to show that on the day of the drownings she did not know the difference between right and wrong. She did seem to be aware of what she was doing, and after the killings she called her husband to tell him what she had done. Although Dr George Ringholz, a neuropsychologist from Baylor College of Medicine, testified that she was severely ill, in the course of an acute psychotic episode, and 'did not know the actions she took on that day were wrong', the prosecution was able to argue that in fact she did know that what she had done was morally wrong.

Among the points of interest in this case is the burden on the defense of proving that at the time of the killings Andrea did not *know* she was committing a crime or doing something that is wrong. Why does the defense have this burden? Couldn't someone be so insane as to be *incapable* of not committing a horrible crime while at the same time knowing that it is a crime? Does the mere fact that one knows that something is morally wrong suffice to show that one is not insane when one does that thing? Just to ask the question is to invite a negative answer! Where then does this important point in the Texas law come from? According to Jennifer S. Bard, a lawyer who teaches at the Institute for the Medical Humanities of the University of Texas Medical Branch at Galveston,[9] when Daniel M'Naghten was acquitted by reason of insanity in the murder of the English prime minister's secretary during an attempted assassination, Queen Victoria called for a reappraisal of the law. The result, adopted in both England and in American courts, made the insanity plea to rest upon the question of whether the defendant *knew* his conduct was wrong. 'Unless a person was so out of touch with reality that he didn't know he was committing a crime, he could be found criminally responsible despite suffering from severe mental illness.'[10]

---

[9] 'Unjust Rules for Insanity', *New York Times*, 13 Mar. 2002, A27.   [10] Ibid.

In the 1970's, a more realistic standard was adopted by many states, including Texas. Even if the defendant knew the conduct was wrong, he could not be found guilty if he had been 'incapable of conforming his conduct' to the requirements of the law. This standard recognized that as a result of mental illness an individual might know he or she is doing wrong but lack the ability to keep from doing it.[11]

It's apparent from this change that 'the power to do otherwise' is here recognized as important to the question of guilt and punishment. Why then was Andrea Yates found guilty simply on the grounds that she knew that what she was doing was wrong? The answer, according to Bard, is that the law in Texas was changed back to the 'did the person know that the behavior is wrong criterion' after the attempted murder of President Reagan by John Hinckley. Hinckley,

shot and wounded the president and three other men in 1981. Mr. Hinckley's acquittal by reason of insanity in 1982 shocked the nation. The next year Texas dropped the element of 'incapable of conforming his conduct' and reverted to a strict 'knowledge-based' standard almost like the old M'Naghten rule.[12]

It's clear that had the Texas law not been changed after the attempt on President Reagan's life, Andrea Yates's case would have been a good deal stronger. As it was, all that the prosecution needed to focus on was showing that she *knew* that what she was doing was wrong. As Bard notes: 'Her plea of not guilty by reason of insanity would have been highly persuasive if the standard were her ability to conform her conduct to the law.'[13]

One can appreciate the difficulty of a jury coming to the conclusion that on the day of the drownings Andrea Yates was simply incapable of conforming her conduct to the law. For while it may be reasonably inferred from her conversation with her husband—both before and after the killings—that she knew that killing her children was morally wrong, how can one determine that at the time she drowned her children she was *unable* to refrain from deciding to drown them? There is reason to think that she would have refrained from killing them had she wholeheartedly willed or chosen not to do the act. It isn't her *physical* ability to control the motions of her limbs that is in question here. Rather, it is what Edwards would call her *moral* ability to effectively choose not to kill them that is at question. To answer that question the

---

[11] Ibid.   [12] Ibid.   [13] Ibid.

jury would have to confront the problem of determining whether her fateful decision to drown them was an irresistible decision or simply a decision she refused to resist. Nevertheless, even though it may be extremely difficult to determine whether her decision to drown them was irresistible, rather than simply not resisted, it certainly appears to be directly relevant to whether she should or should not be severely punished for what she did. For if her decision to drown her children on that day was compelled by mental torment beyond her ability to bear, then in all justice we would have to conclude that she was unable 'to conform her conduct to the law.' And this would be so even though it may also be true that she would have refrained from drowning her children had she willed not to kill them. For her ability to will not to kill her children may have been severely diminished by the mental torment that caused her to choose to drown them. Thus, our first criticism of Edwards's view that moral inability to refrain from willing as one did is *irrelevant* to the agent's moral responsibility for so willing and acting is that it is not in accord with current moral standards. We do take into account a person's inability not to choose as one did in assessing that person's responsibility for so choosing and acting.

I turn now to an objection to Edwards's account of what it is to have the power to do otherwise. He tells us that a drunkard who willingly drinks the cup of alcohol is *free* in that action (and morally responsible for it) provided he had the power to refrain from drinking the cup of alcohol should he will to refrain from drinking it. Moreover, as we've seen, he tells us that it does not matter that the drunkard is *unable* to will to refrain from taking the cup of alcohol and drinking it. All that matters is that were he to will not to take the cup and drink from it he would have the *physical power* to refrain from picking up the cup and drinking from it. And, of course, we admit that the drunkard has the physical power to refrain from drinking the cup of alcohol. What he lacks is the power *to will* to refrain from taking the cup and drinking from it. Hence, it is clear that Edwards takes the *meaning* of 'being free with respect to X-ing' to be 'having the power to X should we choose (will) to X'. Thus he says: 'And the contrary to liberty, whatever name we call that by, is a person's being hindered or unable to conduct as he will, or being necessitated to do otherwise' (II. 5). In short, where 'X' picks out some action, it is clear that Edwards takes both the common meaning of 'S is free to do X' to be 'S can do X if S wills to do X,' and the common meaning of 'S is not free to do X' to be 'S cannot do X if S wills to do X'.

A difficulty with this account, as we saw in the Andrea Yates case, is that it supposes—what may be false—that the agent has the power to determine her will. At one point in his discussion, perhaps sensing the need to respond decisively to this objection, Edwards tries to neutralize the objection by arguing that it is *impossible* that the agent should lack control over his volitions.

And if it be improperly said, that he cannot perform those external voluntary actions, which depend on the will, 'tis in some respect more improperly said, that he is unable to exert the acts of the will themselves; because it is more evidently false, with respect to these, that he can't if he will: for to say so, is a downright contradiction: it is to say, he *can't* will, if he *does* will. And in this case, not only is it true, that it is easy for a man to do the thing if he will, but the very willing is the doing; when once he has willed, the thing is performed; and nothing else remains to be done. Therefore, in these things to ascribe a non-performance to the want of power or ability, is not just; because the thing wanting is not a being *able*, but a being *willing*. (I. 4)

The most plausible reading of this passage is that in response to the objection, 'It's all very well to say that the agent can do X if he wills to do X, but what if he can't will to do X?', Edwards felt some need to do more than assert (his standard response) that it doesn't matter whether the agent has control over his will, that the only question of importance is whether the agent can do *what* he wills. So, in order to put an end to the troubling question, 'But what if he can't will to do X?' Edwards here proposes that the question is *senseless* because it supposes something that is actually a contradiction in terms: that a person who wills to bring it about that he wills some particular action X could possibly fail in that endeavor. For it is a contradiction to suppose that a person who wills to do X doesn't in fact will anything at all. Therefore, since it cannot possibly be true that you both will something and yet don't will anything at all, the question 'What if he can't will to do X?' is senseless.

The mistake in Edward's argument here is not overly difficult to detect. The question at issue is whether the agent has it in his power to will to do some particular action A. Of course, the agent may well have the power to will that he will to do A. But just as an agent who wills to do A may yet fail to do A, so an agent who wills to will to do A may yet fail to will to do A. It is clear, therefore, that there is no contradiction in someone willing that he will to do A and yet failing to will to do A. Edwards's effort to avoid the objection is unsuccessful.

Perhaps Edwards's strongest argument against the Arminians is his argument that God's necessary goodness and the necessity of his always doing what he sees to be best does not prevent the Arminians from insisting, along with the Calvinists, that it is fitting to thank God and praise him for always doing what is best for him to do. Clearly, the Arminians cannot have it both ways. They can't support the view that the *necessity* of God's always doing what he sees to be best is compatible with his being praised and thanked for always doing what he sees to be best, and then reach the opposite conclusion when it comes to evaluating human beings, holding that unless the human being could have done otherwise than he did it makes no sense to thank that person or praise him for doing the good act that he did. God cannot do otherwise than what he sees to be best. Yet we praise him and thank him for so doing. Moreover, the Arminian holds that it is right and proper to thank God and praise him for doing the best, even though he cannot fail to do so. Well then, why insist that a human being must have been able *not* to do the good act if he is to be praiseworthy for doing that good act? Indeed, if there is any reason for discriminating between God and the human moral saint with respect to who it is more reasonable to praise and be thankful to for doing what he sees to be best, the reason falls out in favor of the human moral saint. For in the case of the human moral saint, whose goodness is such that he is now unable to fail to choose the best that he can do, his present inability to do less than the best he can is the result of earlier efforts on his part, efforts that were not necessitated, but freely chosen. Thus, even though the human moral saint cannot now fail to choose the best that he can do, it is by virtue of his own effort over time that he cannot now fail to choose the best that he can do. He is, therefore, 'derivatively' responsible for his present good act. He is presently praiseworthy for having earlier made himself such that he cannot now fail to pursue the best course of action. In the case of God, however, it is not true that God ever could fail to do what he sees to be best. Nor did he ever choose to bring it about that he is presently unable to do less than the best. So, it is difficult, to say the least, to explain how it could be that God is now even 'derivatively' responsible for his present good act. For he never could do other than what he sees to be best. The failure of the great proponents of freedom without causal or logical necessity—for example, Samuel Clarke and Thomas Reid—to provide for libertarian freedom in God with respect to his always doing what is best is a serious defect in their otherwise significant efforts to give an account of divine and human freedom that escapes the difficulties inherent in the necessitarian view of Jonathan Edwards.

Sometimes a fundamental disagreement between able, even great, philosophers is more like ships passing in the night than titans colliding with one another on the field of battle. Such seems to be true of Edwards's most basic criticism of the libertarian theory of freedom presented by Samuel Clarke (whom Edwards read) and Thomas Reid (whom Edwards did not have the opportunity to read). The central idea in Clarke and Reid may be put like this: the soul (person) has a self-determining power by which it determines the will—i.e., brings it about that the soul (person) wills to do something (perform some action). But, so the objection goes, to freely determine an act of will is to freely will that act of will. So an act of will is freely determined only if it is freely chosen. But an agent freely chooses an act of will only if his choice of that act of will is itself freely determined by the agent, in which case the choice of the act of will must be the result of a prior free choice by the agent. And so we are off to the races, each free determination of the will by the agent being preceded by an infinite series of determinations of the will by the agent. Thus Edwards remarks: 'Therefore, if the will determines all its own free acts, the soul determines all the free acts of the will in the exercise of a power of willing and choosing; ... And therefore if the will determines all its own free acts, then every free act of choice is determined by a preceding act of choice, choosing that act' (II. 1). This objection, which Reid traces to Hobbes, fails, however, because it supposes that what it is for the agent to freely determine his will (that is, bring it about that he wills X rather than something else) is for the agent to freely *will* that his will be determined in a certain manner. But it is very doubtful that any free will advocate held this view. Many libertarians attributed to the agent a power of self-determination, a self-moving principle. But by this they meant only that, when the volitional act is produced by the self-moving principle, it is produced by the agent herself and not by any other thing or agent.[14] They did not mean that in causing her volition the agent first chose or willed to produce that volition. To attribute such a view to them is simply to misunderstand what they claimed or, at least, intended to claim. According to the free will advocates, the soul or mind determines the will but does not do so by

---

[14] See 'Unpublished Letters of Thomas Reid to Lord Kames, 1762–1782', collected by Ian Simpson Ross, *Texas Studies in Literature and Language*, 7 (1965), 51.

choosing or willing that the soul (mind) will a certain act rather than some other act. To freely bring about a volition is nothing more than for the agent to exert her power to cause that volition. The exertion of power is not itself a volition.

On Reid's theory of agent-causation, when an agent wills some action, the act of will is itself an event and, as such, requires a cause. If the act of will is free, its cause is not some event, it is the agent whose act of will it is. Being the agent-cause of the act of will, the agent must have had the power to cause that act of will, the power to refrain from causing it, and *exerted her power to cause it*. It is the last condition (an exertion of active power) that leads to an infinite regress if it too is understood as an event requiring a cause. What is reasonably clear in Reid's work is that he did not view an exertion of active power as an event requiring a cause. His most careful statement of a general principle of causation is this:

Everything that begins to exist, must have a cause of its existence, which had power to give it existence. And every thing that undergoes any change, must have some cause of that change. (603)[15]

From this principle it follows that if a being *undergoes a change* then either that being itself is the efficient cause of the change it undergoes, or some other being is the efficient cause of the change, in which case the being undergoing the change is merely passive, acted upon, the active power being only in that being that produced the change. When an exertion of active power occurs in an agent, that exertion is not viewed by Reid as an event requiring a cause. So, for Reid, when we cause our volitions (acts of will) we do so by exerting our active power to produce them. Hence, the occurrence of a volition is an event requiring a cause. But the exertion of active power by which the agent causes that volition is not itself an event requiring a cause. If the exertion of active power by which an agent causes a volition were itself an event requiring a cause, the theory of agent-causation would involve an infinite regress of causes of the sort Edwards notes. Reid's principle requires that for any being that begins to exist there must be a cause. But an exertion of active power is not a being (substantial thing). Nor is an exertion of active power by an agent an instance of that agent undergoing a change. Rather, it is an exercise by the agent of its active power, an exertion that may be

---

[15] Unless stated otherwise, references to Reid's work are to pages of the 1983 printing by Georg Olms Verlag of *The Works of Thomas Reid, D.D.* (7th edn.), ed. Sir William Hamilton (Edinburgh, Maclachlan and Stewart, 1872).

explained by the agent's intentions and purposes. But such intentions and purposes, on Reid's view, do not cause an agent's exercise of active power.[16]

Although Reid's presentation of agent-causation escapes (in my judgment) the infinite regress argument proposed by Edwards, it is not successful, I believe, in providing a satisfactory account of divine freedom. For agent-causation is essentially a two-way power: a power to cause (not-cause) some state of affairs. But given that God sees that bringing about some state of affairs is the best thing (all things considered) for him to do, God *necessarily causes* that state of affairs to be actual. Indeed, if it were in his power not to cause that state of affairs to be actual, it would be in his power to do less good than he can. But it cannot be in God's power to do less good than he can. For if it were, it would be in his power to cease to be perfectly good. And, being necessarily perfect, it cannot be in God's power to cease to be perfectly good.

Of course, none of the considerations just described would deter Edwards from ascribing freedom to God. For Edwards does not require a power to do otherwise as essential to freedom. If a being is free to do as he wills, then, according to Edwards that being is free in doing what he wills. It doesn't matter that the being in question is unable to will and do otherwise. So, for Edwards, God is perfectly free in always acting in accord with what he sees to be the best course of action. But could God fail to do what is best? Could God do evil? Edwards has no difficulty in saying that God could. For *if* God willed to do less than the best, he clearly would have the power to do as he wills, to do less than the best. Never mind that it is *impossible* for God to will to do less than the best. God is free to do evil in so far as he has the power to do so if he were to will to do so. Never mind that it is impossible for God to will to do evil. It is only in some such Pickwickian sense that Edwards can say that God has power to do other than what he sees to be best.

---

[16] For more on this matter see *Thomas Reid on Freedom and Morality* (Ithaca, NY: Cornell University Press, 1991).

5

Must God Create the Best World?

Thus far we have supposed with Leibniz that among possible worlds there is one that is best. And we have argued that given God's absolute perfection, he would of necessity create the best world. If the reasoning for this conclusion is correct, then in the matter of creating among possible worlds God cannot be free. However, as with many important philosophical arguments, the reasoning that has led us to the conclusion that God necessarily creates the best world has been challenged. And in this chapter we will consider an important challenge to this reasoning. Of course, one way of challenging the reasoning is to reject the initial claim that among possible worlds there is one that is best. Perhaps there is no best possible world. Instead, so the suggestion goes, there may be an infinite number of possible worlds ranked in order of goodness such that for any world there is a world better than it. We will discuss this challenge in the next chapter and consider the implications of the 'no best world' hypothesis for the existence of the theistic God. But the challenge to be discussed here is quite different. For it allows that there may be a best possible world, but maintains that even if there is a best world God would not need to create it. Instead, so the claim goes, he might create some good world that is considerably less good than the best world. But before examining this challenge it will be helpful to have a clearer idea of just what a possible world is, as well as a clearer idea of what it is for a possible world to be better than some other possible world.

Up to this point we have assumed, what I believe is correct, that we all possess some rudimentary idea of what a possible world is and what it would be for one such world to be better than any other possible world.

But as we get deeper into our subject it will be necessary to develop a clearer understanding of these concepts. So, before pursuing the question of whether God must create the best possible world, it will be helpful here to pause in our discussion and try to get clearer about the notion of a possible world and some related concepts.

Often we think that although things are a certain way they didn't have to be that way, they could have been different. We were late getting to class today, but, so we believe, things could have turned out differently. Had we not stopped on the way to chat with a friend, for example, we almost certainly would have been on time. So, what we may call the *actual* state of affairs, our being late for class, need not have been actual at all. Here then we make a distinction between two possible states of affairs—ways things might be—and note that although one is actual (our being late for class today), the other (our being on time for class) was possible, it could have been actual instead. The link between possible states of affairs that are not actual and our common ways of thinking about the world lies in our frequent belief that things could have been otherwise. Whenever we correctly think that things could have gone in a way different from the way they actually went, we are distinguishing between some possible state of affairs that is actual (the way things did go) and some possible state of affairs that didn't become actual (the way things could have gone but didn't). Every state of affairs that is actual is clearly a *possible* state of affairs, one that, logically speaking, could be actual. But, as we've seen in the example of our not being late for class, possible states of affairs may fail to be actualized. Perhaps, then, we should think of a possible state of affairs as one that could be actual and could fail to be actual. But this view overlooks a useful distinction philosophers draw between a state of affairs that is *possible* and a state of affairs that is *contingent*. A contingent state of affairs is a possible state of affairs that may be actual or fail to be actual. Since a possible state of affairs is one that could be actual, if it is also such that it could fail to be actual (like, for example, our being on time for class today), then it is a *contingent* state of affairs. It can be actual and can fail to be actual. But some states of affairs are such that although they are possible, and therefore can be actual, they cannot fail to be actual, they *must be* actual. These possible states of affairs are necessary, not contingent. Consider the state of affairs consisting in the number 3's being larger than the number 2. Certainly, this state of affairs is possible—it's not like there being an object that is both square and round, an impossible state of affairs. So, it is a possible state of affairs. But is it contingent? Could it have failed to be actual. No. The number 3's being larger than the number 2 is not just possible, it is also necessary, it obtains in every possible world. So, while many possible states of affairs are contingent in that they obtain in some worlds but not in others,[1] many possible states of affairs are necessary, they obtain in every possible world. The following diagram shows the way philosophers often distinguish among states of affairs.

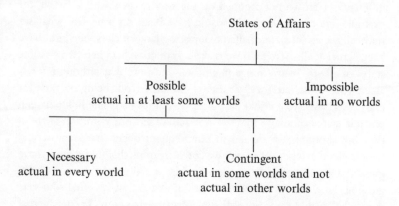

In order to grasp the idea of a *possible world* it is helpful to consider two important relations among states of affairs: *inclusion* and *preclusion*. A state of affairs S *includes* a state of affairs S^* just in case it is impossible that S should obtain and S^* not obtain. (For example, *Gordie Howe's being the greatest hockey player of the twentieth century* includes *someone's being the greatest hockey player of the twentieth century*.) S precludes S^* just in case it is impossible that S obtain and S^* obtain. (So, *Gordie Howe's being the greatest hockey player of the twentieth century* precludes *Wayne Gretsky's being the greatest hockey player of the twentieth century*.) Following Alvin Plantinga, we can now say what it is for a state of affairs to be *maximal* and, therefore, a *possible world*. 'A State of affairs S is . . . *maximal* if for every state of affairs S', S includes S' or S precludes S'. And a possible world is simply a possible state of affairs that is maximal.'[2]

---

[1] In saying that a state of affairs *obtains* (or is *actual*) in a given possible world we mean that that state of affairs would be actual were that world the actual world.

[2] Alvin Plantinga, *The Nature of Necessity* (Oxford: Oxford University Press, 1974), 45.

Having seen that a possible world is a *maximal* state of affairs, we can now consider what it is for a possible world to be better than some other possible world. Some states of affairs may be said to be intrinsically better than other states of affairs. To repeat the example of Samuel Clarke's, noted in Chapter 2, we may say that *there being innocent beings who do not suffer eternally* is necessarily better than *there being innocent beings who do suffer eternally.* Of the second of these two states of affairs we would say that it is a bad state of affairs, something that ought not to be. But the first state of affairs is not a bad state of affairs. The basic idea here is that some states of affairs possess intrinsic value. That is, they may be intrinsically good, intrinsically bad, or intrinsically neutral (neither good nor bad). They are intrinsically good by virtue of containing intrinsically good qualities such as happiness, love, enjoyment, beauty, good intentions, or the exercise of virtue.[3] And states of affairs are intrinsically bad by virtue of containing intrinsically bad qualities such as unhappiness, hate, dissatisfaction, ugliness, bad intentions, or the exercise of vice. Still other states of affairs, may contain little or no intrinsic value. *There being stones*, for example, is a state of affairs that contains little if any intrinsic value. Such states of affairs are, we might say, intrinsically neutral. But *someone's being happy*, for example, is an intrinsically good state of affairs, while *someone's being unhappy* is an intrinsically bad state of affairs.

One might infer from the preceding paragraph that if God exists, the world he creates would be composed of nothing but intrinsically good states of affairs.[4] However, supposing it would be in God's power to create such a world, there are at least two reasons to question this inference. First, as theodicists have argued since the time of Augustine, freedom of the will, if not itself a great intrinsic good, appears to be indispensable for some of the very important goods we know of—freely given love, freely sacrificing for the well-being of others, freely chosen

[3] See Roderick M. Chisholm, 'The Defeat of Good and Evil', in Marilyn McCord Adams and Robert Merrihew Adams (eds.), *The Problem of Evil* (Oxford: Oxford University Press, 1990). Also, see the explication of this concept in G. E. Moore, *Principia Ethica* (Cambridge: Cambridge University Press, 1903).

[4] Actually, since possible worlds necessarily exist, God doesn't create them. But from the fact that a possible world exists, it doesn't follow that it is *actual*. Only one world can be the actual world. And what God does is create particular things—stones, human beings, etc.— and enable them to be arranged in such a way that a particular possible world is actualized. So, it is not in the literal sense of 'creates' that God creates a world. With this understood, we will continued to refer to some possible world as being 'created' by God.

acts of charity, etc. Indeed, from the point of view of the creator it might well be uninteresting to create beings who are programmed from the start to worship God, to honor him, to do good to others. From the perspective of the creator it may well be better to have beings who can freely choose to love and worship or not to love and worship, for love and worship that is freely given is of much greater value than love and worship that is compelled. But if God does choose to create a world with creatures free to do good or evil, the world may include evil as a result of some of their free choices.[5] Second, there is a principle, *the Principle of Organic Unities*,[6] held by a number of philosophers from Leibniz to the present day. According to this principle, the intrinsic value of a whole may not be equal to the sum of the intrinsic value of each of its parts. Compare, for example, *Jones's feeling happy upon contemplating torturing an innocent human being* with *Jones's feeling unhappy upon contemplating torturing an innocent human being*. The difference between these two states of affairs is that the first contains an intrinsically good state (Jones's feeling happy) as a part, whereas the second contains an intrinsically bad state (Jones's feeling unhappy) as a part. But surely the first state as a whole is a much worse state of affairs than the second. For, while a given part of a whole may be intrinsically good (Jones's feeling happy), the whole of which it is a part may be worse for the presence of the good part than it would be were a certain bad part (Jones's feeling unhappy) to be in its place. So, for all we know, the best world may include some intrinsically bad states of affairs. It hardly follows from this consideration that there may be tears in heaven, but it does suggest that we should hesitate to conclude too much from the mere presence of some tears on earth. For, as we've seen, a state of affairs that constitutes an *organic unity* may be better for the presence of a bad part than it would be were the bad part replaced by a good part. So, again, we must note that a possible world with some bad parts may be better than a possible world with no bad parts.

We've seen that the good-making qualities (happiness, love, enjoyment, beauty, good intention, an exercise of virtue, etc.) figure in states of affairs (e.g., someone's being happy, someone's loving another, etc.) that are intrinsically good; whereas the bad-making qualities (unhappi-

---

[5] But surely there would be possible worlds in which creatures are free to do good or evil and, as it happens, always use their freedom to do good. Wouldn't God create one of those worlds? For an impressive argument as to why it might not be in God's power to create such a world see Plantinga, *Nature of Necessity*, ch. 9.

[6] See G. E. Moore, *Principia Ethica*, 187 ff.

ness, hate, dissatisfaction, ugliness, bad intentions, or the exercise of vice) figure in states of affairs (e.g., someone's being unhappy, someone's hating another, etc.) that are intrinsically bad. It is important, however, to distinguish the *intrinsic* value of someone's being unhappy from the *extrinsic* value of someone's being unhappy. The intrinsic value of a state of affairs is inherent in that state of affairs—it necessarily belongs to that state of affairs no matter what that state of affairs is a part of or what the circumstances are in which it occurs. But the extrinsic value of a state of affairs may change from one set of circumstances to another. Sometimes, for example, a person's being unhappy is productive of good, in which case it may be a good thing (i.e., it may be extrinsically good) for that person to be unhappy. But that doesn't affect the matter of the intrinsic value of someone's being unhappy. For it is a good thing that the person was unhappy only in the sense of what that person's unhappiness leads to, not in terms of its own intrinsic value. Unhappiness, in itself, is always bad. In addition, we should not confuse the intrinsic value of a state of affairs with the intrinsic value of a state of affairs of which it is a *part*. As we've noted someone's being unhappy on contemplating the undeserved suffering of others is a better state of affairs than someone's being happy on contemplating the undeserved suffering of others. But that truth is entirely compatible with someone's being happy necessarily being *intrinsically better than* someone's being unhappy. For the intrinsic value of the part, someone's being unhappy, must not be confused with the intrinsic value of the whole (someone's being unhappy on contemplating the undeserved suffering of others) of which it is a part.

Since a possible world just is a *maximal* state of affairs, its value will reflect the values of the states of affairs contained in it. So, possible worlds themselves will be intrinsically good, intrinsically bad, or intrinsically neutral. In addition one possible world will be intrinsically better than, equal to, or worse than another possible world. And, as Leibniz noted, it is by knowing the intrinsic values of the possible worlds that God is guided in his choice of a world to create.

We can now take up the objection to Leibniz's view that God would be lacking in wisdom, goodness, or power were he to choose to create any world less than the best possible world. In an important article, Robert M. Adams argues that it need not be wrong for God to create a world that is not as good as some other world he could create.[7] Adams

---

[7] Robert M. Adams, 'Must God Create the Best?', *Philosophical Review*, 81 (1972), 317–32.

supposes that the world God creates contains creatures each of whom is as happy as it is in any possible world in which it exists. Moreover, no creature in this world is so miserable that it would be better had it not existed. Adams then supposes that there is some other possible world with different creatures that exceeds this world in its degree of happiness, a world that God could have created. So, God has created a world with a lesser degree of happiness than he could have. Has God wronged anyone in creating this world? Adams argues that God cannot have wronged the creatures in the other possible world, for merely possible beings don't have rights. Nor can he have wronged the creatures in the world he has created, for their lives could not be made more happy. Adams notes that God would have done something wrong in creating this world were the following principle true.

> It is wrong to bring into existence, knowingly, a being less excellent than one could have brought into existence.[8]

But this principle, Adams argues, is subject to counter-examples. Parents do no wrong, he points out, when they refrain from taking drugs that would result in an abnormal gene structure in their children, even though taking the drugs would result in children who are superhuman both in intelligence and in prospects for happiness. As opposed to the incorrect principle just cited, Adams does support the more plausible principle:

> It is wrong for human beings to cause, knowingly and voluntarily, the procreation of an offspring of human parents which is notably deficient, by comparison with normal human beings, in mental and physical capacity.[9]

From these sensible observations concerning what would be right or wrong for humans to do in producing offspring, Adams infers that God would not be doing something wrong in bringing into existence humans who are less excellent than he could have brought into existence. But before we accept this inference, we should note an important difference between God's situation in considering creating human beings and the situation of parents who are considering taking drugs in order to bring into existence children who are superhuman both in intelligence and in prospects for happiness. In the latter case there is an inherited background of existing children who are brought about in normal ways and

---

[8] 'Must God Create the Best?', 329.
[9] Ibid. 330.

who establish what is *normal* with respect to human intelligence and prospects for happiness. Against this established background both of normal ways of producing children and of what is *normal* in the way of intelligence and prospects of happiness, it is quite sensible to conclude that parents are under no *obligation* to produce non-normal children who are *superhuman* both in intelligence and in prospects for happiness. For we cannot help but think that they would be producing beings who would be strangely different, if not estranged, from much of the human race, the humans who are *normal* both in intelligence and in prospects for happiness. But in creating human creatures it is God himself who establishes what the norm of human intelligence will be and what the prospects for human happiness will be. There is no already existing norm from which God may choose to deviate either by creating beings who are subhuman or superhuman in the way of intelligence and prospects of happiness. Within the limits of what it is to be human it is up to God to set the norm for human intelligence and prospects for happiness. And if we suppose there is a lower and upper limit for *human* intelligence and happiness, the question is whether God would be doing something wrong in creating humans whose prospects for intelligence and happiness are rather low, or in the middle, given that he could have created other humans with prospects for a considerably higher level of intelligence and happiness. We grant that God may not have wronged the humans he did create, since, as Adams supposes, *they* could not have been created with any greater prospects for a good and happy life. But it remains difficult to see how God would be justified in creating creatures whose prospects for a good life are known by him to be mediocre in comparison with other creatures of the same species whose prospects for a good life are known by him to be much greater—given that this knowledge is all that is relevant to God's decision about which creatures to create. In my judgment, Adams's analogy fails to address this more serious question and, by implication, fails to address the serious question of whether God would be obligated to create the best world.

Suppose, however, that we set aside whatever disagreements we may have with Adams on these points and accept the conclusion of his reasoning. Suppose, that is, that we agree with Adams that God is not *morally obligated* to create the best world that he can, that it would be morally permissible for God to create the best world he can, but also morally permissible for God to create any of a number of other good worlds of the sort Adams describes. If so, can't we conclude that there is no unresolvable conflict between God's being essentially morally perfect and his enjoying a significant degree of genuine freedom? For it now appears that God's moral perfection does not require him to create the best world. In short, he is free to create (or not create) any of a number of good worlds.

As forceful and persuasive as Adams's arguments may be, I don't think they yield the conclusion that God's perfect goodness leaves God free to create less than the best world that he can create. What Adams's arguments show, at best, is that God's moral perfection imposes no *moral obligation* on God to create the best world he can. His arguments establish, at best, that God need not be doing anything *morally wrong* in creating some world other than the best world. But this isn't quite the same thing as showing that God's perfect goodness does not render it *necessary* that he create the best world he can. For, even conceding the points Adams makes, there still may be an inconsistency in a morally perfect being creating some world other than the best world he can create. My point here is this. One being may be morally better than another even though it is not better by virtue of the performance of some *obligation* that the other failed to perform. It may be morally better by virtue of performing some *supererogatory act*—a good act beyond the call of duty—that the other being could have but did not perform. Analogously, a being who creates a better world than another being may be morally better, even though the being who creates the inferior world does not thereby do anything wrong. Following Philip Quinn, I'm inclined to think that if an all-powerful, all-knowing being creates some world other than the best world it can create, then it is possible there should exist a being morally better than it is.[10] For it would be possible

---

[10] Philip L. Quinn, 'God, Moral Perfection, and Possible Worlds', in Frederick Sontag and M. Darrol Bryant (eds.), *God: The Contemporary Discussion* (New York: The Rose of Sharon Press, Inc., 1982), 197–213. Quinn remarks: 'An omnipotent moral agent can actualize any actualizable world. If he actualizes one than which there is a morally better, he does not do the best he can, morally speaking, and so it is possible that there is an agent morally better than he is, namely an omnipotent moral agent who actualizes one of those morally better worlds' (213). We should note that my version of Quinn's principle is presented in terms of the overall goodness of a world, not just its moral goodness. Thus, my version of the principle states that if an omniscient being creates a world when there is a better world it could create, then it would be possible for there to be a being morally better than it. I do not, as Quinn does, focus solely on the *moral* status of a world. For some good states of affairs include nonmoral goods such as happiness, as well as moral goods such as the exercise of virtue. It could be, however, that the difference is merely terminological, for Quinn may hold that the *moral status* of a world depends on both the moral and nonmoral good the world contains.

for there to be an omnipotent being who creates the best world that the first being could create but did not. Shouldn't we then conclude that if an essentially all-powerful, all-knowing, perfectly good being creates any world at all, it must create the best world it can? For although a being may do no wrong in creating less than the best it can create, a being whose nature is to be *perfectly good* is not such that it is possible for there to be a being morally better than it. If, however, a being were to create a world when there is a better world it could create, then it would be possible for there to be a being morally better than it.

The heart of Adams's essay, however, proposes a reason for rejecting the view we have just stated: that if a being were to create a world when there is a better world it could create, then it would be possible for there to be a being morally better than it. For the view we have come to implies, in Adams's words, that 'the creator's choice of an inferior world must manifest a defect of character'. And his response to this objection is that 'God's choice of a less excellent world could be accounted for in terms of His grace, which is considered a virtue rather than a defect of character in Judeo-Christian ethics.'[11] It is Adams's understanding of the Judeo-Christian view of grace that lies at the core of his objection to the Leibnizian view that the most perfect being 'cannot fail to act in the most perfect way, and consequently to choose the best'. So, any answer to Adams's view that God need not choose to create the best world must take into account his view that the Judeo-Christian view of grace implies that God may create a world less than the best.

Adams defines the concept of grace as 'a disposition to love which is not dependent on the merit of the person loved'.[12] Given this definition and given two worlds, W1 and W2, that differ in that the persons in W1 are happier and more disposed to behave morally than are the persons in W2, with the result, let us suppose, that W1 is a better world than W2, it is clear that a gracious God would not love the persons in W1 more than the persons in W2. Or, at the very least, it is clear that were God to love the persons in W1 more than the persons in W2 it would not be because they are morally better and/or happier. As Adams remarks: 'The gracious person loves without worrying about whether the person he loves is worthy of his love.'[13] So, by virtue of his grace, either God would love all persons to an equal degree or the fact that he might love one person more than another would have nothing to do with the fact

[11] 'Must God Create the Best?', 318–19.   [12] Ibid. 324.   [13] Ibid.

that the one has a greater degree of merit or excellence than another. As Adams puts it: 'the gracious person sees what is valuable in the person he loves, and does not worry about whether it is more or less valuable than what could be found in someone else he might have loved.'[14] And he tells us that in the Judeo-Christian tradition grace is held to be 'a virtue which God does have and men ought to have'.[15]

Given that grace is as Adams has defined it and that grace is a virtue God possesses, what may we infer about the world God creates? Can we infer with Leibniz that if there is a best world God must create that world? It is difficult to know what to say here. All that we've learned from Adams thus far is that it would be something other than *love* that would motivate God to choose the best world, or any other world for that matter. For since grace is a disposition to love without regard to merit, God will be unable to select one world over another if all he has to go on is his grace. His grace (love toward creatures independent of their degree of merit) will leave him free to create any world that has creatures able to do moral good or evil, regardless of how good or bad they may be in that world. So, if God has a reason to choose one creaturely world over another—rather than blindly picking one out of the hat, so to speak—that reason will have little or nothing to do with his grace. For given the doctrine of grace, God's *love* for creatures is not based on the quality (moral, religious, etc.) of the lives they lead; and it is difficult to see what else about their lives it could be based on. In fact, the implication of the Judeo-Christian doctrine of grace for God's selection of a world to create seems to be entirely negative—rather than giving a reason why he might select a particular creaturely world, or rule out other creaturely worlds, it simply tells us that if God creates a world with creatures, his love of the creatures in that world cannot be his reason for creating it. For his love for creatures is entirely independent of who they are and the kind of lives they lead. To base his love on who they are and the kinds of lives they lead would be to take those persons and their lives as more deserving of his love than other persons and their lives.

What we've seen thus far is that God's grace—his love of creatures without respect to their merit—cannot provide God with a reason to create the best world, or any particular world less than the best. And what this means is that whatever reason God has for choosing to create one creaturely world over another cannot be found in his gracious love

---

[14] 'Must God Create the Best?', 324.   [15] Ibid.

for creatures.[16] In what then, given that God has a reason for creating one world over another, would that reason reside? It would reside not in God's gracious love but, I suggest, in his desire to create the very best state of affairs that he can. Having such a desire, I believe, does not preclude gracious love. It does not imply that God cannot or does not equally love the worse creatures along with the best creatures. Let me explain by using an analogy of my own. Loving parents may be disposed to love fully any child that is born to them, regardless of whatever talents that child is capable of developing. But such love is consistent with a *preference* for a child who will be born whole, without mental or physical impairment, a child who will develop his or her capacities for kindness toward others, who will develop his or her tastes for music, good literature, etc. And in like manner, God will graciously love any creature he might choose to create, not just the best possible creatures. But that does not rule out God's having a preference for creating creatures who will strive as creatures not only to have a good life but also to lead a good life, creatures who will in their own way freely develop themselves into 'children of God'. Indeed, although God's gracious love extends to every possible creature, it would be odd to suggest that he, therefore, could have no preference for creating a world with such creatures over a world in which creatures use their freedom to abuse others, use their talents to turn good into evil, and devote their lives to selfish ends. Surely, God's graciously loving all possible creatures is not inconsistent with his having a preference to create a world with creatures who will use their freedom to pursue the best kind of human life. How could he not have such a preference? Furthermore, as I've suggested, if God had no such preference, his gracious love for creatures would give him no reason to select any particular possible world for creation. For his gracious love for each and every creature fails to provide a reason to create one creature rather than another, or to create the creatures in one possible world rather than those in another. So, if God is not reduced to playing dice with respect to selecting a world to create, there must be some basis for his selection over and beyond his gracious love for all creatures, regardless of merit. And that basis, given God's nature as an absolutely perfect being, can only be, as Leibniz and Clarke maintained, to do always what is 'best and wisest' to be done. And surely

[16] For further argument in support of this point see Mark L. Thomas, 'Robert Adams and the Best Possible World', *Faith and Philosophy*, 13 (1996), 252–9.

the best and wisest for God to do is to create the best world he can. Moreover, doing so seems to be entirely consistent with God's gracious love of all creatures, regardless of their merit.

Adams, however, flatly rejects the view I've just described, a view that sees God's gracious love of creatures without respect to merit as entirely consistent with his having an all-things considered preference to create the best world he can. After noting that divine grace is love which is not dependent on the merit of the person loved, Adams proceeds to draw the conclusion that although God would be free to create the best creatures, he cannot have as his *reason* for choosing to create them the fact that they are the best possible creatures.

God's graciousness in creating does not imply that the creatures He has chosen to create must be less excellent than the best possible. It implies, rather, that even if they are the best possible creatures, that is not the ground for His choosing them. And it implies that there is nothing in God's nature or character which would require Him to act on the principle of choosing the best possible creatures to be the object of His creative powers.[17]

By my lights, God's disposition to love independent of the merits of the persons loved carries no implication as to what God's *reason* for creating a particular world may be, other than that his reason cannot be that he *loves* the beings in this world more (or less) than the beings in other worlds. And, of course, having an all-things considered preference for creating the best world need not be rooted in a *greater love* for beings who are better than other beings. As we've seen, owing to the Principle of Organic Unities, the best whole may have some parts that are not the best. Therefore, the best world may contain some human beings who are not better than, or even as good as, their replacements in the closest world to the best world. And God may select creatures to create who will choose to grow morally and spiritually, rather than creatures who will choose not to grow morally and spiritually, and select them for that very *reason* without his thereby *loving* the former persons more than the latter, or loving them because of their greater merit. God's grace does rule out choosing to create the best world because he *loves* its inhabitants more than the inhabitants of some lesser world. But it does not rule out God's choosing to create the best world because he prefers to create the best persons, so long as he does not love them more than he

---

[17] 'Must God Create the Best?', 324.

loves the inhabitants of lesser worlds. Adams, of course, must be supposing that if God's reason for creating one world rather than another is the fact that the creatures in the first world are much better than the creatures in the second world, it somehow logically follows that God must love the creatures in the first world more than he loves the creatures in the second. But there is nothing in his presentation of the view that God's love for creatures is independent of their merit that yields this result. I conclude, therefore, that we have been given no good reason to think that the Judeo-Christian concept of grace rules out the view of Leibniz and Clarke that God must create the best.

6

Divine Perfection and Freedom: The Contemporary Debate

On the assumption that among the possible worlds there is a best world, we have considered the alternatives facing God as creator. And we have reached the preliminary conclusion that God's absolute perfection would leave him no choice other than the choice to create the very best world. In the course of reaching this conclusion we've looked with some care at the writings of Leibniz and Samuel Clarke, both of whom hold that there is a best possible world, and we've concluded that neither succeeds in the effort to avoid the conclusion that God's choice to create the best world is *absolutely necessary*. But since it seems impossible to prove that there is a best among possible worlds (or a best world creatable by an infinitely powerful, infinitely wise being were such a being to exist), we must now consider the apparent possibility that there is no best world, that for any world creatable by God (if he exists) there is a better world he could create instead.[1] If this were the way things are, it seems initially reasonable to suppose that while God would not be free to create a bad world he would be free to create some good world even though he could create a better world instead. For on the supposition that for every creatable world there is a better creatable world it would be impossible for God to create a world that is better than any other creatable world. But against this initially reasonable supposition—that God would create a good world even

---

[1] I ignore here the other possibility: there being several equally good worlds and none better. This possibility is briefly discussed later in the chapter.

though there are better worlds he could create—we've noted that it conflicts with what appears to be a very plausible principle:

> *if an omniscient being creates a world when there is a better world it could create, then it would be possible for there to be a being morally better than it.*

Since God is a being than which it is not possible for there to be a morally better being, it is clear, given both the principle just cited and the no best world hypothesis, that God could not exist and be the creator of a world. For any being that exists and creates a world when there is a better world it could have created instead is, according to the principle cited above, a being than which a morally better being is possible, and, therefore, not the best possible being. So, the issue now before us is whether this principle [*if an omniscient being creates a world when there is a better world it could create, then it would be possible for there to be a being morally better than it*] is indeed true. My own view is that the principle in question will appear to many to be plausible, if not self-evident. For if an omniscient being creates a world when it could have created a better world, then that being has done something less good than it could do (create a better world). But any being that knowingly does something (all things considered) less good than it could do falls short of being the best possible being. So, unless we find some reason to reject the principle stated above or a reason to reject the line of argument supporting it, we are at the very least within our rights to accept it and use it as a principle in our reasoning. But the result of using this principle in our reasoning about God and the world is just this: if the actual world is not the best world that an omnipotent, omniscient being could create, God does not exist. God does not exist because were he to exist and create a world when there is a better world he could have created instead, then he would be a being than which a better being is possible. For he himself would have been a better being had he created a better world. But since it is not possible for any being (including God) to be better than God (the best possible being) in fact is, the world God has created must be the very best world he could have created. Therefore, if God does exist and creates a world W, W is the very best among the worlds that God could have created. W is the best creatable world. Hence, we see the problem of no best creatable world. For if our principle (cited above) is true and for every creatable world there is a better creatable world, God does not exist. What then can be said against the principle: *if an omniscient being creates a world when there is a better world it could create, then it would be possible for there to be a being morally better than it?*

I

We may begin by considering again the view set forth by Norman Kretz-mann in his study of Aquinas's view of creation.[2] In the course of his discussion of Aquinas, Kretzmann concludes with Aquinas that for any world God might create there is a better world he could create. (His disagreement with Aquinas concerns only whether God is free not to create at all.) Kretzmann's second conclusion—the one presently of inter-est to us—is that it is a *mistake* to think (as I do) that if God exists and cannot avoid choosing something less good than he could choose, then God cannot be essentially perfectly good. And he proceeds to explain why he thinks it is a mistake.

Like Aquinas, I think that the logical truth that God's actions conform to the principle of noncontradiction entails no limit on his power. And if it would be a violation of the principle of noncontradiction for God to create a world better than any other world he could create, then a fortiori that logical truth which does not diminish his power also leaves his *goodness* undiminished. God's being that than which nothing better can be conceived of cannot entail his producing a world than which none better can be conceived of. No matter which possible world he actualizes, there must be infinitely many possible worlds better than the actual world in some respect or other.[3]

Kretzmann relies on what he takes to be an analogy or parallel between power and goodness. His idea is this. Since we agree that failure to bring about what is logically impossible does not imply any limit on God's power, we should also agree that failure to bring about what is logically impossible does not diminish God's goodness. Given that there is no best world, Kretzmann points out that it is logically impossible for God to create a world better than any other world he could create. So, the fact that God does not create such a world diminishes neither his power nor his goodness. And that being so, Kretzmann sees no difficulty in God's being perfectly good and creating a world less good than other creatable worlds.

Perhaps we can view Kretzmann as appealing to the following principle:

---

[2] Portions of this chapter have been taken (with permission of the editor of *Faith and Philosophy*) from my essay 'Can God Be Free?', *Faith and Philosophy* (Oct. 2002), 405–24.

[3] 'A Particular Problem of Creation', 238.

A. If S is a logically impossible state of affairs, then the fact that a being does not bring about S does not entail that the being in question lacks power or perfect goodness.

This principle strikes me as self-evidently true. The fact that God fails to do what *logically cannot be done* is a bad reason to think that God is morally imperfect or lacking in power. On Aquinas's view it is logically impossible for God to create the best possible world. And since he cannot do that, the fact that he doesn't do it, as Kretzmann notes, implies no imperfection in God. I entirely agree with Kretzmann's point on this. But the fact that there is a bad reason to conclude that God is not perfectly good does not mean that there is no good reason to conclude that God is not perfectly good. And the fact that God fails to do what *logically can be done* may be a good reason to conclude that God is not perfectly good.[4] The principle that provides this good reason is the principle we've already introduced and will now refer to as 'Principle B.'

B. If an omniscient being creates a world when there is a better world that it could have created, then it is possible that there exists a being morally better than it.[5]

If B is true, as I think it is, and if it is also true that

C. If a being is essentially perfectly good then it is not possible that there exist a being morally better than it,

then if it is true that for any creatable world there is another creatable world better than it, it is also true that *no* omnipotent, omniscient being who creates a world is essentially perfectly good. Moreover, if we add to this Kretzmann's first conclusion that a perfectly good, omnipotent, omniscient being *must* create, it will follow that there is no omnipotent, omniscient, perfectly good being.

II

Suppose Aquinas and Kretzmann are right in believing that for any creatable world there is another creatable world that is better than it.

---

[4] In this discussion of Kretzmann I suppose, for effect, that it is possible for God to be less than perfectly good. What is true is that any being that fails to do what is the best it can do is not perfectly good and, therefore, not God.

[5] As we noted earlier, a being may be perfectly morally correct in the sense of never failing in its obligations and still be such that it could be morally better by virtue of the performance of some supererogatory act.

Our second objection emerges when we consider what the theistic God is to do in this situation. If some creatable world is better than any world God alone inhabits, then, on my Principle B (slightly extended) it appears that God must create some world. On the other hand, as we've just seen, on my Principle B it also follows that he cannot create a world if some other creatable world is better. 'So', the objector now concludes, 'on your Principle B it follows that God must create a world and also must not create a world. Surely, then, since your principle leads to a contradiction, however plausible Principle B sounds, we must reject it.'

My response to this objection is that on the supposition that for every creatable world there is another world that is better than it, Principle B does not lead to a contradiction. What Principle B leads to is the conclusion that there is no essentially omnipotent, omniscient, perfectly good being.

But is Principle B true? Daniel and Frances Howard-Snyder have endeavored to refute Principle B by inviting us to consider three hypothetical world creators: Jove, Juno, and Thor.[6] They suppose Jove to be an omnipotent, omniscient being who is confronted with an infinite number of increasingly better possible worlds from which to select one to create. Jove, they suggest, decides to create one of these good worlds by using a randomizing device. Being good, Jove has no interest in creating a world that isn't good.[7] Each of the infinite number of good worlds is assigned a positive natural number beginning with '1' for the least good world, '2' for a slightly better world, and so on. Jove uses the randomizing device to pick one of these good worlds, and, as a result, world no. 777 is created. Now, of course, Jove could have created a better world. But the Howard-Snyders think that it does not follow from this fact that Jove is *morally surpassable*. That is, from the fact that Jove could have created a better world than the world he did create (no. 777), they think that it does not follow that it is *logically possible* for there to have existed a being with a degree of moral goodness in excess of Jove's.[8]

In a response to their article[9] I suggested the following:

[6] Daniel and Frances Howard-Snyder, 'How an Unsurpassable Being Can Create a Surpassable World', *Faith and Philosophy* (Apr. 1994), 260–7. Further references to this article will appear in the text.

[7] In order not to beg the question at issue, the Howard-Snyders do not assume that Jove is morally unsurpassable.

[8] In the context of this discussion, a being is morally unsurpassable only if it is logically impossible for there to be a morally better being.

[9] 'The Problem of No Best World', *Faith and Philosophy* (Apr. 1994), 269–71.

In support of their view the Howard-Snyders invite us to consider other possible omnipotent, omniscient[10] world creators, Juno and Thor, and argue that although they produce morally better worlds than Jove, they are not morally better creators. Juno does just what Jove did but her randomizing machine happens to select a better world, no. 999. Thor doesn't use a randomizing machine but selects world no. 888 over Jove's world no. 777 because he sees that it is better and prefers creating no. 888 to creating any lesser world. Even though Juno ends up producing a better world than Jove, the Howard-Snyders are clearly right in viewing Jove and Juno as morally equivalent. For had her randomizing machine hit on world 777, rather than world 999, Juno would have created world 777. So, it was blind luck, not a higher standard of selection, that resulted in Juno's selection of world 999. But what of Thor? From their discussion it would seem that Thor is morally superior to Jove and Juno, for it looks as though Thor's degree of moral goodness is such that he is not prepared to settle for world no. 777 *unless* he is unable to create a better world. But the fact that Jove intentionally included worlds numbered 1–777 as possibilities for selection by his randomizing machine shows that Jove is morally prepared to settle for any of the worlds from 1–777 *even though* he is able to create a better world.[11] So, it does appear that, other things being equal, Thor is a morally better being than Jove.[12]

I noted earlier that our authors do not explicitly make Juno and Thor epistemically equivalent to Jove. This is unfortunate for it leads them to impute a principle of action to Thor that cannot possibly apply to an omnipotent, omniscient being who chooses to create from among infinitely many progressively better worlds. Thus they say:

> The important point to see here is that given a choice between infinitely many progressively better worlds to create, Jove wisely rejects Thor's principle that if there's a better world than w, don't create w, . . . because that principle in that context would lead him (and Thor, were he rational) to do nothing, which is far worse than using the randomizer. (264)

But if the principle in question, 'if there's a better world than w, don't create w,' *were* Thor's guiding principle, then Thor could not be omniscient and create anything—for, as the authors say, Thor is facing

---

[10] For some reason the Howard-Snyders neglect to attribute omniscience to Juno and Thor. I assume this to be a slip. Clearly, if we want to compare their goodness to Jove's, we should attribute to them the infinite power and knowledge that was attributed to Jove. I'll return to this point in discussing Thor's degree of goodness.

[11] And the same is true of Juno, even though she accidentally ends up with world no. 999.

[12] It is important to note that to say one being is morally better than another is not to imply that the second being has done anything morally wrong or violated any moral obligation.

'Jove's choice', the choice of selecting among infinitely many progressively better worlds. But once we do provide a level playing field for Thor and Jove, specifying that Thor, like Jove, is *omniscient* as well as omnipotent, we see that *given his selection of world no. 888*, no such principle can be motivating Thor. (For, knowing that he must select among infinitely many progressively better worlds, such a principle would prohibit Thor from creating the world he does create, no. 888.) Rather, Thor's degree of moral goodness presumably is such that he is prepared to settle for world no. 888, but not prepared to settle for the world (no. 777) that Jove's degree of moral goodness allows him to settle for. We thus have reason to believe that Thor's degree of moral goodness exceeds Jove's, that Thor is morally better than Jove.

What the Howard-Snyders may have shown is that the fact that one omnipotent, omniscient being creates a world that is morally inferior to the world that another such being would create does not show, *by itself*, that the first being, other things being equal, is morally inferior to the second. (For, as they note, the selection of a world to create may be the result of a random process.) What they have not shown, I believe, is that an omnipotent, omniscient being who creates a world morally inferior to another world it could have created can be morally unsurpassable.

In a subsequent article[13] against Principle B, the Howard-Snyders question my account of Thor, suggesting that it is incoherent. They wonder what principle or reason Thor acts on. They say:

For example, suppose Thor's reason is this: worlds numbered 888 and higher are better than worlds numbered 887 and lower. (This seems to be the reason that Rowe has Thor act on. See the quotation above.) This reason relies on the general principle that if world w is better than world w − 1, then w − 1 is unacceptable for creation. Any being who accepted an instance of this principle when it involved the world no. 888 but did not accept other instances of it would be irrational, and hence not essentially omniscient. Any being who accepted the principle in its full generality would be led never to create, given (as we are supposing) that for each world there is a better.[14]

This leads them to suggest that my account is *incoherent*. But I believe it is clear from my article that I do not have Thor act on the principle 'don't create if there is a better creatable world', for such a principle, given that for any world there is a better, can only result in Thor's not creating any world at all. Since Thor is *omniscient* and does in fact create world 888, it

---

[13] 'The *Real* Problem of No Best World', *Faith and Philosophy* (July 1996), 422–5.
[14] Ibid. 423.

logically follows that he cannot act on the principle that they suggest I have him act on. Of course, while Thor, given his infinite intelligence, cannot act on such a principle, it doesn't follow that with finite intelligence I cannot make the mistake of attributing to Thor such a principle of action when he creates world 888. So, what principle do I have Thor act on? I believe that the principle on which Thor acts is very much like the principle on which Jove acts. Let's look again at Jove. Some worlds he sees as not good enough to be acceptable as candidates for creation. The worlds that are acceptable to him in terms of his own degree of goodness are then ordered in terms of increasing goodness, and one of them, world 777, is randomly selected for creation. Thor, as I have described him, does pretty much the same thing. The difference is that worlds 1–800 are insufficiently good to be acceptable to him as candidates for creation, given that there are better worlds he can create. The worlds that are acceptable to him in terms of his own degree of goodness are then ordered in terms of increasing goodness and one of them, world 888, is randomly selected for creation. I conclude that the description the Howard-Snyders give of Jove is logically consistent with there being a being who is better than Jove. And the story we have told about Thor is consistent and, if true, gives us reason to believe that Thor is a better being than Jove.

Can we state the principles on which both Jove and Thor act, and explain how it is that although they act on the same principles, they produce worlds that differ in their degree of goodness? I suggest that Jove and Thor may act on the following principles:

P1. Do not create any world that is not a good world.
P2. Do not create any good world whose goodness is less than what one judges as *acceptable*, given that one can create a better world.[15]

Clearly, both Thor and Jove act in accordance with P1 and P2. Neither is prepared to create a less than good world. And neither is prepared to create a good world whose degree of goodness is less than what he judges as acceptable in a world, given that he can create a better world.

---

[15] I use the expression 'acceptable world' to pick out a world that a knowledgeable world creator may choose to create given that creator's own degree of goodness and given that it is in that creator's power to create an even better world instead. Of course, if there is a best world to create, two creators may differ in their respective degrees of goodness as creators and yet both choose to create the best world. But when confronted with an infinity of increasingly better creatable worlds, a creator with a lessor degree of goodness will see some creatable worlds as acceptable for creation that a creator with a greater degree of goodness will reject as unacceptable.

The difference between them is this. Jove's standard of goodness in world creating is such that he is prepared to settle for *any* good world even if there is a better that he can create. Thor, however, has a higher standard. He is not prepared to create any of the good worlds from W1 to W800 provided there is a better world that he can create. Of course, Thor's allegiance to P2 does not preclude him absolutely from creating, say, W777. It prevents him only on the condition that there is a better world he can create. Gala apples taste much better than Jonathan apples. I know that, and my standard of apple selection is never to come home with Jonathan apples when Gala are available. But that doesn't mean I won't or can't select Jonathan apples when Gala apples are not available. A good apple, even if it's a Jonathan, is better than no apple at all.

In their article the Howard-Snyders suppose that it cannot be that Thor and Jove act on the *same* principle. They suppose that if my story about Thor being better than Jove is correct then Thor must be acting on a *higher principle* than the principle on which Jove acts. And, since there will be worlds better than the world Thor creates, they then conclude that 'there is another principle which treats as unacceptable some of the worlds which were treated as acceptable by Thor's principle, and that other principle is such that there is a third principle which treats as unacceptable some of the worlds which were treated as acceptable by the second, and so on, *ad infinitum*'. Lacking a proof of the impossibility of such an infinite array of world-creating principles, they say,

It seems odd to say the least that there should be infinitely many such general principles. At least we see no reason to accept that there are.[16]

As I've tried to make clear above, the story I tell is quite consistent even if there is no such infinite progression of world-creating principles. Principles P1 and P2 will suffice so long as for any being in the position of Jove or Thor there is another being whose degree of goodness is such that its application of P1 and P2 results in the selection of a better world to create. And if we allow, as the Howard-Snyders do, an infinite number of possible worlds beginning with Jove's good world W1, why not allow

---

[16] I use the expression 'acceptable world' to pick out a world that a knowledgeable world creator may choose to create given that creator's own degree of goodness and given that it is in that creator's power to create an even better world instead. Of course, if there is a best world to create, two creators may differ in their respective degrees of goodness as creators and yet both choose to create the best world. But when confronted with an infinity of increasingly better creatable worlds, a creator with a lessor degree of goodness will see some creatable worlds as acceptable for creation that a creator with a greater degree of goodness will reject as unacceptable, 424.

the possibility of an infinite series of good world creators each being better than the preceding one. Indeed, why not allow, if needed, an infinite number of different but related world-creating principles. But, as I've suggested, I don't see the necessity of supposing that my story is coherent only if there is an infinite number of distinct world-creating principles. But suppose an infinite number of such principles is required. Perhaps it is odd at that there should be infinitely many world-creating principles. But even if it is odd, we should note that oddness and impossibility are far different matters. Many extremely odd things are logically possible. And if it is logically possible that there is an absolutely infinite number of increasingly better worlds, why should it be impossible that there be an infinite number of principles of world creation? In any case, however, I see no reason to think that there need be an infinite number of such principles in order for the story of Thor and Jove to be coherent. Indeed, I have suggested that Jove and Thor can act on the very same principles. Moreover, since it is possible that there be world creators whose degrees of goodness increasingly exceed Thor's, it is possible that the very same principles would result in increasingly better beings creating increasingly better worlds than Thor's world.

The fundamental question at issue in the discussion concerning Jove and Thor is this: Is it logically possible both that for any creatable world there is a better creatable world and that there exists an omnipotent, omniscient, perfectly good being who creates one of these creatable worlds? My position is that it is not possible that both should be true. Why do I hold this position? I hold it because, as I've stated earlier, I think the following [Principle B] is necessarily true.

B. If an omniscient being creates a world when it could have created a better world, then it is possible that there be a being morally better than it.[17]

By telling their story about Jove, the Howard-Snyders hoped to cast doubt on Principle B. I believe that my alternative story about Thor undermines their attempt. Where does this leave us? I assert that B is necessarily true. Many theists assert the following [Principle A] to be true.

A. It is logically possible both that for any creatable world there is a better creatable world and that there exists an omnipotent, omniscient, perfectly good being who creates one of these worlds.

---

[17] *Indeed, it is possible for that very being to have been better than it in fact is.*

Both of us cannot be right. But how can we hope to settle the question of who has the more plausible position? Are we simply at a stalemate, a situation where neither can show the other's position to be implausible without employing as a premiss one of the principles that is at issue in the debate? I believe that the Howard-Snyders have endeavoured to advance the debate in a way that does not beg the question. They suppose both that Jove is an omnipotent, omniscient creator of a good world (no. 777) and that for every creatable world there is a better, but leave as an open question whether Jove's goodness can be unsurpassable. The question then is whether we have some good reason to think that an omnipotent, omniscient creator of a better world than no. 777 may be better than Jove. As we've seen, the answer depends on the reason such a being has for creating a better world than no. 777. If such a being (their Juno), given her degree of goodness, judges as acceptable for creation the same worlds as Jove, then the fact that her randomizer selects world no. 999 for creation gives us no reason at all to think that Juno is a better being than Jove, even though she ends up creating a better world than does Jove. But if, like Thor, the being's degree of goodness is such that he judges that worlds of lesser value than no. 800 are unacceptable candidates for creation, then the fact that its randomizer selects world no. 800 or higher gives us reason to think that Thor is a better being than Jove. Of course, if we had simply concluded that Jove's goodness is surpassable because Jove could have created a world better than no. 777, this would have been to beg the question at issue. For we would have been appealing to Principle B to rule out Jove being an unsurpassably good being. But no such appeal was made in reasoning to the conclusion that Thor is a better being than Jove.

Principle B, if true, does not refute theism. But if both Principle B and theism are true, then the world we live in is an unsurpassably good world—no possible world that an omnipotent being could have created would be better than the actual world. I suspect that part of the motivation for the theist to accept the view that there is no best creatable world is that the alternative seems both to limit severely God's freedom in creating, and to leave the theist with the burden of defending the Leibnizian thesis that this world, with all its evil, is a world than which a better creatable world is not even a logical possibility.

III

Thomas Morris, like the Howard-Snyders and Kretzmann, thinks that among the worlds creatable by God there is no best world. He notes two difficulties in the Leibnizian idea that there is a best possible world. First, he points out that some philosophers are doubtful that there is a single scale on which all creaturely values can be weighted so as to determine what world possesses the maximum amount of value. 'Some world A might be better than rival world B in some respects, but with B surpassing A in others, and the relevant values not such that they could be summed over and compared overall.'[18] In short, if some valuable states of affairs are incommensurable with other valuable states of affairs, it may be impossible to rank the states of affairs in terms of one being better than, worse than, or equal to the other. And if that should be so, we could have two worlds such that neither is better than the other, worse than the other, or equal in value with the other. Second, Morris notes that a number of philosophers have thought that for any world containing 'a certain number of goods, n, there is always conceivable a greater world with $n + 1$ goods, or good creatures. So, on the simplest barest grounds of additive value alone, it seems impossible there could be a single best possible world. And without this, of course, the Leibnizian demand collapses.'[19] But Morris's main concern lies elsewhere. Like the Howard-Snyders and Kretzmann, Morris wants to show that there is no incoherence in the idea of a *perfectly* good creator creating a world when there is no best world for that being to create.

For just as it seems initially very natural to suppose that a superlatively good, wise, and powerful being will produce only an unsurpassable perfect creation, so likewise it can seem every bit as natural to suppose that an incoherence or impossibility discovered in the latter notion indicates an incoherence or impossibility buried within the former.[20]

Since it is just that incoherence we have been arguing for, it is important to note Morris's efforts to show that the incoherence in question is imagined, and not real. Noting that Quinn holds that in the no best world scenario a creator of a world is such that 'it is possible that there is

---

[18] 'Perfection and Creation', in Eleonore Stump (ed.), *Reasoned Faith* (Ithaca, NY: Cornell University Press, 1993), 234–47.

[19] Ibid. 237.

[20] Ibid.

an agent morally better than he is, namely an omnipotent moral agent who actualizes one of those morally better worlds', and I hold that 'if a being were to create a world when there is a morally better world it could create, then it would be possible for there to be a being morally better than it', Morris observes that these views are 'absolutely unacceptable to traditional theists, for whom both perfection and creation are important ideas'.[21]

In developing his objection to the views expressed by Quinn and Rowe, Morris introduces a useful thesis—the *Expression Thesis: The goodness of an agent's actions is expressive of the agent's goodness.* I'm inclined to think that something like this thesis is related to the claim expressed in Principle B: If an omniscient being creates a world when it could have created a better world, then it is possible that there be a being morally better than it. Of course, the Expression Thesis depends on what Morris may well have supposed: that the agent's motive for performing the good action is to bring about a good state of affairs. Without supposing that motive we have no reason to think that the goodness of an agent's action—measured in terms of the quality of its result—is expressive of the agent's goodness. But what are we to say of a being who performs an action that he knows will result in the world's being considerably less good, all things considered, than it would be were he (at no cost to himself) to perform a slightly different action? In this case, applying the Expression Thesis, we should conclude that the agent's degree of goodness is something less than it could be. For the agent has acted to bring about less good than he knew would have been brought about by his performing a slightly different action. But clearly, if a world creator knowingly acts to bring about less good overall than he could have brought about by performing a slightly different action, that creator's degree of moral goodness is somewhat less than it could be. And it is precisely this point that underlies the judgment that in the no best world scenario it is impossible for the omniscient creator to be perfectly good. For, as we saw in the discussion of the Howard-Snyders' story about Jove, Juno, and Thor, when a being creates a world that is less good than another world it could have created, the world it creates will satisfy its standard of world-creating, even given that it could create a better world. But then it is *possible* that there should be a being whose degree of goodness is such that it will not create that less good world given that it is able to

[21] 'Perfection and Creation', in Eleonore Stump (ed.), *Reasoned Faith* (Ithaca, NY: Cornell University Press, 1993), 239.

create a better world. So, again I conclude that if a being creates a world when it could have created a better world, then it is *possible* that there should be a being morally better than it. And from this it follows that if for every creatable world there is a better creatable world, there is no absolutely perfect being who creates a world. And since it is better to create a good world rather than not create any world at all, on the no best creatable world scenario there is no maximally perfect being.

Morris's basic mistake, I believe, is his view, shared by Kretzmann, that to hold, as I do, that if there is no best world for a being to create then no being can create a world and be a being than which a better creator is impossible, just is to hold God accountable for not doing what is logically impossible to be done—creating the best world. Thus Morris writes:

> If you and I do less well than we're capable of doing, then those around us may conclude, and may sometimes justifiably conclude, that we are not at the level of goodness that could be exemplified. But failing to do the best you can is a flaw or manifests an incompleteness in moral character in this way only if doing the best you can is at least a logical possibility. If doing the best he can in creating a world is for God an impossibility, . . . then not doing his best in creating cannot be seen as a flaw or as manifesting an incompleteness in the character of God. The notion of a perfect expression of an unsurpassable character would then itself be an incoherence.[22]

Of course, if it is logically impossible for there to be a best world, then God's not creating the best possible world does not count against his perfect goodness. Nowhere do I suggest that it does. What counts against God's perfect goodness (specifically, his moral perfection) is his creating a world when he could have created a world better than it. The charge is not that a being who fails to do what is impossible to be done (create the best world when there is no best world to be created) is lacking in perfect goodness. The charge is that a being who creates a world when it could have created a better world is less than supremely perfect. And the plain fact is that if there is no best creatable world then God, if he creates a world, will create a world than which he could have created a better world.[23] Morris simply fails to address the issue at stake here.

---

[22] 'Perfection and Creation', 244.

[23] This is technically incorrect. For if there is no best world, but several worlds equally good and none better, then a being could freely chose one of these worlds to create. The reader is to understand that in supposing that there is no best world we are here thinking only of the circumstance in which for every world there is a better world.

It is important to distinguish three different principles:

(a) Failing to do the best one can is a defect only if doing the best one can is possible for one to do.

(b) Failing to do better than one did is a defect only if doing better than one did is possible for one to do.

(c) Failing to do better than one did is a defect only if doing the best one can is possible for one to do.

Both (a) and (b) are true. But (c) is not true. And it is (c) that Morris needs to make his argument work. Indeed, there is some indication that Morris assumes that (c) is true. For in the passage quoted above he begins by saying:

If you and I do less well than we're capable of doing, then those around us may conclude, and may sometimes justifiably conclude, that we are not at the level of goodness that could be exemplified.

Why does Morris say that those around us may 'sometimes justifiably conclude', rather than 'always justifiably conclude'? The likely answer is that sometimes those around us know that we are aware that there is a best thing that we can do, but we deliberately choose to do less than the best—thus revealing that our goodness is, as it were, less that it could be. For someone who can do the best thing all things considered, but deliberately chooses to do less than the best, manifests a deficiency in goodness. And this answer clearly would allow Morris to *deny* that to do less good than we can, when there is *no best thing* we can do, is to be lacking in goodness. So, the issue to be resolved here is whether a being who knowingly does less good than he can, when there is no best thing he can do, is somehow deficient in goodness.

Suppose, for the moment, that you are an omnipotent, omniscient being and are contemplating the infinite series of numbers: 1, 2, 3, 4, etc., etc. You are also contemplating the infinite series of creatable worlds containing creatures that are overall good worlds, as opposed both to bad worlds and neutral worlds—worlds that are neither good nor bad. You let each of the numbers represent the overall degree of good that a possible world possesses, where '1' represents the least good world—a world with no pain perhaps, and just one momentary experience of pleasure on the part of some lower animal. '2' represents the possible world that is one degree better than the world 1, '3' represents the possible world that is one degree better than the world 2, etc., etc.

Being omniscient you see that there is no best possible world for you to create. Just as the series of natural numbers increases infinitely so does the series of increasingly better worlds from which you will select one to create. Seeing that there is no best possible world to create, you realize that no matter how good a world you create there will be better worlds you could have chosen to create instead of it. Glancing at world 1, and comparing it with world 1000, you see that world 1000 is significantly better than world 1, just as you see that world 1000,000 is significantly better than world 1000. Nevertheless, in spite of noticing the enormous disparity between the least good world and the goodness of some worlds numerically much greater, you decide that you will create the *least good* world and proceed to actualize world 1. Isn't it obvious that in deliberately choosing to create the *least good* of the infinite series of increasingly better possible, creatable worlds you display a degree of goodness in world-creating that is inconsistent with *perfect goodness*?

'Wait!' you will say. 'You judge me unfairly. I see that if I could have created a maximally good world I might be subject to some criticism here for creating a world so limited in value as world 1. But there is no maximally good world. So clearly I'm *perfectly justified* in creating the *poorest* in the infinite series of increasingly better worlds. You should not have any doubts at all about my being *perfectly good*!'

Surely this defense of one's 'perfect goodness' is woefully inadequate. A perfectly good being cannot, consistent with its perfect goodness, consciously elect to create the least good world when there is an infinite number of increasingly better worlds as available for creation as the least good world. But it is just this conclusion that Morris would have us accept. Since the conclusion is clearly false, if not absurd, we should reject it. Instead, we should say that the degree of goodness an omniscient being possesses is reflected in the degree of goodness in the world it creates. And what this reasoning leads us to is the conclusion Leibniz reached: An unsurpassably good, omnipotent, omniscient creator will create an unsurpassably good world. Indeed, unsurpassable goodness in an omnipotent, omniscient world creator is consistent only with the creation of an unsurpassably good world. For there is an impossibility in the idea both that there exists an infinite series of increasingly better creatable worlds and that there also exists an unsurpassably good, omnipotent, omniscient being who creates one of these worlds.

IV

In an important and challenging paper, 'The Freedom and Goodness of God',[24] William Hasker presents a careful and sustained critique of the argument we've given for the conclusion that God, if he exists and creates a world, must create the best possible world.[25] Since he raises objections that we've not thus far discussed, it is important to examine his view in some detail. He begins by agreeing with my remark that 'however much we may succeed in trying to fit the terrible evils in our world into some rational plan, few are prepared to think with Leibniz that this world is as good as any world could possibly be' (2). But what if there simply is no best world for God to create? What if, as Hasker puts it, 'there can be no such thing as the best creatable world' (8)? Following Thomas Morris (see our discussion of Morris above), he then suggests a few reasons for thinking that a best creatable world is an impossibility. But if there is no best world for God to create, then whatever world God does create, he could have done better. And if that should be so, it seems clear to Hasker that God cannot be at fault for failing to create a better world. But since our Principle B:

> If an omniscient being creates a world when there is a better world it could create, then it would be possible for there to be a being morally better than it

does imply that God would be lacking absolute moral perfection were he to create a world when he could have created a better world, Hasker proceeds to consider my defense of Principle B (against the views of both Morris and Kretzmann). Noting that my defense of Principle B in the no best world scenario is this:

> . . . if it is logically impossible for there to be a best world, then God's not creating the best world does not count against his perfect goodness. Nowhere do I suggest that it does. What counts against God's perfect goodness (specifically, his moral perfection) is his creating a world when he could have created a world better than it,

[24] My references (with his permission) are to the pages of a paper Hasker kindly sent to me. The content of the paper is to appear in his book, *Providence, Evil, and the Openness of God*, being published by Routledge. References appear in the text.

[25] Technically, all that is required is that God create a world than which no creatable world is better. For there could be several equally good creatable worlds and none better. But this point is not relevant to Hasker's criticism. So, it may be safely ignored here.

Hasker then considers the three principles I state and distinguish from one another.

(a) Failing to do the best one can is a defect only if doing the best one can is possible for one to do.

(b) Failing to do better than one did is a defect only if doing better than one did is possible for one to do.

(c) Failing to do better than one did is a defect only if doing the best one can is possible for one to do.

As we saw in the discussion of Morris's critique, I hold that (a) and (b) are *true*, whereas (c) is *false*. Hasker thinks I am dead wrong in holding that (c) is false. And he proceeds to offer a proof that (c) is in fact *true*. After noting that 'failing to do better than one did' is to be understood as failing to do a better act one could have done instead of the act that one in fact did, Hasker proceeds to express 'the agent failed to do better than she did' as

$$(\exists x)[Px \,\&\, (\exists y)(\sim Py \,\&\, \Diamond Py \,\&\, y > x)]$$

where x and y are variables taking as values actual or possible actions, $x > y$ is understood as x is better than y, and Px is understood as the agent performs x. So, in English what the formula says is:

There is an action the agent performs, there is an action the agent did not perform, it is possible for the agent to have performed the latter action, and the latter action is better than the action the agent in fact performed.

Using the above symbolic abbreviations, he then provides a formula for the expression: 'doing the best one can is not possible for one to do'.

$$\sim \Diamond(\exists x)[Px \,\&\, \sim (\exists y)(\sim Py \,\&\, \Diamond Py \,\&\, y > x)]$$

In English, what this logical formula says is equivalent (trust me) to the following:

It is necessary that: for any action that an agent performs, there is an action that agent did not perform but was possible for the agent to have performed, and that action is better than the action the agent in fact performed.

So, the latter formula tells us that it is necessarily true that no matter what action an agent performs there is a different action it was possible for him to perform instead, and that different action is better than the action the agent performed. And, clearly, if that is so then doing the best one can is simply not possible for one to do.

Having established the formula for 'doing the best one can is not possible for one to do', Hasker asks: 'If doing the best one can is not possible for one to do, is it *possible*, as Rowe claims, to avoid the "fault" of failing to do better than one did?' (10). He then provides a rigorous proof that it is not possible, and concludes on the basis of this proof that

(c) Failing to do better than one did is a defect only if doing the best one can is possible for one to do

is in fact *true*, contrary to my contention that (c) is false. Summing up, Hasker draws out the implications of his proof.

So, if there is no best possible world, it is impossible for God to avoid the 'fault' of creating a world that is less good than some other world God could create. But a 'fault' that it is logically impossible to avoid is no fault at all; it is not a moral defect. It seems likely that Rowe has been misled by the 'could have done better' locution. It is quite true that, on the assumption of no best world, God has created a world less good than some other world he could have created. The question that needs to be asked, however, is whether this alleged 'fault' is one it was logically possible to avoid. The answer, of course, is that it was not, and so it is not a fault at all. (11)

Let's consider proposition (c).

(c) Failing to do better than one did[26] is a defect (a fault) only if doing the best one can is possible for one to do.

We might compare (c) with the following different principle:

(d) Failing to do better than one did is a defect (a fault) only if doing better than one did is possible for one to do.

The latter principle, (d), is, I think, most certainly true. (c), however, is *false*. Hasker says I am mistaken about this, that (c) is in fact *true*. Why do I say (c) is false? Because even if doing one's best is not possible (for example, creating the best world, given that for any world there is a better), it still may be possible to do better than one did. For, clearly, given that there is no best world (i.e., for every creatable world there is a better creatable world), if an all-powerful being creates a world it will be true

---

[26] The expression 'failing to do better than one did' is here used to imply that the agent in question could have performed a better action than the action he in fact performed—where 'performing a better action' is taken to include refraining from performing any action. Thus when an agent could have performed a better action than the one he did in fact perform we may say that the agent failed to do better than he did. If at the time the agent performed the act he did it was not in his power to have done something better than that action, it is not true that the agent failed to do better than he did.

that he could have created a better world than the one he did create. Suppose, then, that confronted with an infinite array of increasingly better worlds, and no best world, a world creator elects to create the *least good* of this infinite array of increasingly better worlds. We can label the least good world W1. I say that if a world creator creates W1, when he could have created any other world in the infinite array of increasingly better creatable worlds, then a world creator has done less good than he can, and thus manifests a defect in character. [In fact, I would argue that even though W1 is a possible world, it is not creatable by a perfectly good world creator given that he could have created any one of a number of better worlds than it. And I say this even given the assumption that there is no best creatable world, that for every creatable world there is a better.]

Hasker says I'm wrong, for (c) is in fact *true*. Moreover, as we've seen, he not only says that (c) is true, he offers a proof that (c) is true. What he undertakes to prove is this: failing to do better than one did is a *fault* only if doing one's best is possible. Given that there is no best world, that for every creatable world there is a better creatable world, it is impossible for a world creator to do his best in creating a world. Therefore, since it is impossible for a world creator to do his best with respect to creating a world, he cannot be faulted for creating *any* world in the unending series of increasingly better worlds beginning with the least good world. And this means that a world creator can't be faulted for creating even the least good world. For if he creates at all, he cannot avoid creating a world than which there is a better world that he could have created instead.

Who is right here? Hasker says he is right and I, therefore, am wrong. Moreover, he offers a proof in support of his position. I am a bit more charitable on this point than Hasker is. I think we are both right! How can that be? The reason we can both be right in giving opposite answers to what is 'apparently' the same question is that in fact it is not the same question to which we are giving answers. Let me try to explain.

Suppose there is a least good creatable world, W1. And suppose, once again, that there is an infinite array of increasingly better creatable worlds—W2, W3, W4, and so on ad infinitum. This is the 'no best world' scenario. Let us also suppose there is an infinitely powerful, all-knowing creator who can create any single one of the worlds composing this infinite array of increasingly better worlds. Seeing that W1 is the least good world in this infinite array of increasingly better creatable worlds, this being, let us say, selects W1 and creates it. Could this being have created a better world? The answer is obvious. *Yes.* Could it have created a world *than which none is better*. Again, the answer is obvious. *No*. Knowing these things, does this being exhibit any defect or failure in creating the least good world instead of creating some better world in the infinite array of increasingly better worlds? That is the question that Hasker and I are endeavoring to answer. I say that the correct answer is yes. He says the correct answer is no.

Why does Hasker answer this question in the negative? He answers it in the negative because he interprets the question to mean this: Could this being have created a world that is not just better than W1 but is also not subject to the *general defect* of being a world that is less good than some other creatable world? Since the answer to this question is clearly 'No', Hasker concludes that a world creator is not at fault for creating the least good world when he could have created a world enormously better than it. He is not at fault for not creating a much better world than the least good world because any such world would have been subject to the same *general* fault: it too would be a world that is less good than some other creatable world. In short, in Hasker's view, if there is no best world for a world creator to create, a world creator is not at fault for creating the least good world of an infinite array of increasing better creatable worlds. And, as I've said, I think this is the *correct answer* to the following question:

> Could this being have created a world that is not just better than W1 but is also not subject to the *general defect* of being a world that is less good than some other creatable world?

Indeed, so far as I can tell, Hasker's question is just another way of asking whether this being could have created a world than which none is better. In short, Hasker's question (as I have interpreted it) is equivalent to the question: Could this being have created the best possible world? So, in the no best possible world scenario it is not in the least surprising that the answer should be no. But the question I raised is not Hasker's question. Supposing this being creates W1, the question I raised is this:

> Could this being have created a better world than W1?

The answer to this question is, of course, 'Yes'. Although an infinitely powerful, all-knowing being could not have created a perfect world, he could have created any one of a vast number of good worlds, each of which is better than the least good world. And I would think that even if there is no best world, it is, nevertheless, a failing for a being to intention-ally create a minimally good world—a world, say, in which there is some pleasure but none of the higher goods of enjoying beauty, fine music, loving relationships, etc.—when just as easily he could have created a world in which these more significant goods flourished in abundance. And the fact that had he created that better world he would still fail to create an even better world is no reason to think that he isn't at fault for creating the least good world. [Hasker's principle here amounts to this: If you cannot create the best—because there is no best to be created—you do no wrong in creating the least good of all the worlds you can create.] Of course, no matter what world he creates, he will not do the best he can do. For in the no best world scenario, there is no best that the creator can do by way of creating a world. And that does imply that he cannot be at fault for not 'doing' the best he can do. For there is no best for him to do. But what he can do is create a world better than the least good world. So, if he creates the least good world, he will be at fault for failing to create a world better than *the least good world*. Is that a fault he could have avoided? Yes. Had he created a better world than W1 he would have avoided creating the least good world. Would he still be at fault had he instead created a better world than the least good world? Yes. But he would not have been at fault for creating the least good world. Can he create a world and not be at fault for creating *that* world? No. For since there is no best world, he will be at fault no matter what world he creates.

I think Hasker and I agree that a world creator cannot be faulted for failing to create what he cannot create. If there is no best possible world then a world creator cannot be faulted for failing to create it. And if there is no world better than the least good world, then a world creator cannot be faulted for failing to create a world better than the least good world. Where we differ is with respect to this: if there is no best world, can a world creator be at fault for creating *this particular world* when he could have created a better world? I say he can be. Hasker says he cannot be. I think he is wrong. For the mere fact that you cannot create the best world—since there is no such world to create—doesn't somehow make it morally right to create the least good world when there is an infinity of increasingly better worlds any one of which you could have created instead. And if you do create the least good world, you cannot then pass yourself off as a *perfectly good* world creator.

But what of Hasker's proof that if there is no best creatable world one cannot be at fault for creating any world you please, even the least good world? Actually, he doesn't give a proof of this. Instead, he gives a 'proof' of the principle that I hold to be *false*:

    (c) Failing to do better than one did is a defect only if doing the best one can is possible for one to do.

Here is how his proof goes. He begins by asking: 'if doing the best one can is not possible for one to do, is it *possible*, as Rowe claims, to avoid the "fault" of failing to do better than one did?' To show that it isn't possible, Hasker gives a proof that no matter what one did it is possible for one to have done better. He concludes from this that I am mistaken in thinking that in the no best world scenario it is possible to avoid the fault of failing to do better than one did. By my lights he is wrong about this. For suppose this being creates a world. If so, just what does this being create? Does he create *some world or other* than which there is a better? Yes, he does. But can he avoid that 'fault'? No. For in the no best world scenario, no matter what world he creates he will be creating *some world or other* than which there is a better. So, here we must agree with Hasker that it is not a failing to create some world or other than which there is a better. But, of course, no supremely perfect world creator can create a world and do no more than create *some world or other* than which there is a better. For a world just is *a maximal state of affairs*. Therefore, the worlds than which there is a better form a sequence each with its name: W1 is the least good world; W2 is the world than which any less good world is W1; W3 is the world than which the less good worlds in order of decreasing goodness are W2, W1; W4 is the world than which the less good worlds in order of decreasing goodness are W3,W2, W1, etc. To create a world one must create a *particular world*, not just some world or other. So, to suppose that God has created some good world less good than W3 just is to suppose that God created W2 or God created W1. With this in mind, suppose God creates a world. Suppose that world is W3001. Our question, then, is *not* whether God has created 'some world or other' than which there is a better. If, somehow, that is *all* he did, Hasker would be right. No matter what world he creates he will not have avoided creating 'some world or other' than which there is a better. But what God did is create W3001. And here it is not true that no matter what world he creates he will not have avoided creating W3001. For if, instead of creating W3001, God creates W3002, W3003, or some still better world, God will not create W3001, although he will create a world better than W3001. So, if God creates W3001, God could have avoided the *fault* of failing to create a world better than the one (W3001) he did create.

Suppose that Mary must choose a spouse from a long line of eligible bachelors. Indeed, let us suppose that Mary has no choice in this matter: she is coerced into picking a man to marry. And she is coerced into picking a man from among the long line of eligible bachelors. (We may also suppose that Mary has a dossier on each of the bachelors in the line. So, her decision is informed, not blind.) She slowly walks along the line, pausing every now and then, and finally selects bachelor number 56 in the line of eligible bachelors. While she was not free to avoid selecting some man or other from the long line of eligible bachelors, she was free to pick some man other than number 56. Is Mary responsible for picking man number 56? Yes. Is Mary responsible for picking some man or other from the long line of eligible bachelors? No. Similarly, given that it is better to create a world than to create no world at all, God is not subject to criticism for creating *some world or other* from the series of creatable worlds. But he surely may be subject to criticism for creating, say, the least good world when he could have created instead a much better world. And matters won't change if there is no best world for God to create. Of course, Hasker is right. God isn't subject to criticism for creating *some world or other* than which there is a better. For given that it is better to create a world than not to create at all, God is doing the right thing in choosing to create a world rather than not creating at all. And since it is impossible for God to create a world (in the no best world scenario) and yet not create a world than which there is a better he could have created instead, God cannot be faulted for creating *some world or other* than which there is a better. Given that it is better to create a world than not to create a world, he couldn't do otherwise than create some world or other. And given that he couldn't do otherwise than create some world or other than which there is a better, he can't be criticized for creating some world or other than which there is a better. But suppose he then creates W1, the least good world. Can he be at fault for creating world W1? Yes. For he could have done better than create W1. Indeed, there is no limit to his doing better in creating a world other than the least good world. And given that there is no best world, he will be at fault no matter which *particular world* he selects to create in the unending series of increasingly better worlds. So, because of his necessary existence and maximal perfections, God must create a world and yet (in the no best possible world scenario) cannot create a world without doing less good than he can. Small wonder, then, that both Leibniz (the compatibilist) and Samuel Clarke (the libertarian) agreed that there must be a best possible world for God to create.

Against the argument just presented, it is tempting to reply as follows:

But what if a perfectly good, omnipotent, omniscient being exists and just finds himself in the following situation: he sees that there is an infinite number of increasingly better possible worlds and no best world. Suppose also that this being knows that it is better to create a good world than not to create at all. What is the being to do? Surely, being good he will chose to create a very good world, a world, nevertheless, than which there is a better possible world that he could have created instead. If this is so, isn't it simply a mistake to then claim that this supremely perfect being isn't really perfect after all? For to so claim is to hold him to blame for something he was simply not able to do: create a world than which there is no better creatable world.

What we've come to see is that this reply supposes that each of two internally consistent propositions is consistent with the other. The two propositions are:

> There exists an omnipotent, omniscient, perfectly good being who creates a world

and

> For any creatable world there is a better creatable world.

And the principle that enables us to see the inconsistency is Principle B: *If an omniscient being creates a world when there is a better world that it could have created, then it is possible that there exists a being morally better than it.* For suppose a being selects a world W1 to create when there is a better world W2 it could have created instead. Surely it is logically possible that there be a being whose degree of moral goodness is such that when confronted with worlds W1 and W2, either of which it has the power to create, it will choose to create W2, the better world. And this would then be a better being than the being whose degree of goodness permitted it to select the less good world to create when it could have as easily created the better world.

In 1988 a one paragraph article appeared in the journal Analysis. Written by Stephen Grover of All Souls College, Oxford, it elegantly expresses the incompatibility embodied in the two propositions: *There exists an omnipotent, omniscient, perfectly good being who creates a world* and *For any creatable world there is a better creatable world.*[27] Here is the article in its entirety.

---

[27] There is this difference between Grover's account and mine. Grover allows that God *randomly* chooses a world to create from the infinite series of increasingly better creatable worlds. I suggest that God creates a world only if it is *acceptable* to him for creation given his own degree of goodness. But the outcome of our respective arguments is the same.

Leibniz claimed that if there were no best of all possible worlds, God would not have created any world at all. This can be defended in the following way: suppose there is no best of all possible worlds, but only an infinite series of possible worlds, each marginally better than the last. An omnipotent God could create any member of this series, whereas a 'weak god', of great but not quite unlimited power, could create many, but not all, of the members of the series. Whichever member of the series God randomly chooses to create, it will be possible that the world He chooses is not as good as the world which a weak god would, if he existed, choose to create. This possibility is incompatible with the claim that God is perfectly good, for that claim must entail the claim that there is no other imaginable agent who could ever act in a way that is morally better than the way in which God acts. It may not impugn God's goodness to say that He could have acted better than He in fact did, but it surely impugns His goodness to say that some other imaginable being could have done so. The easiest way in which this possibility can be excluded is to claim that there is no possible world better than the world which God chooses to create. Either this is the best of all possible worlds, or God is not omnipotent, not perfectly good, or does not exist.[28]

V

We are now in a position to consider what is perhaps the most probing of the responses to the view here argued for: that the existence of an omnipotent, omniscient, perfectly good being who creates a world is inconsistent with the supposition that for every creatable world there is a better creatable world. In 'Jonathan Edwards, William Rowe, and the Necessity of Creation',[29] William Wainwright notes that the Christian tradition has, by and large, ascribed libertarian freedom to God. He then suggests that there is some motive for doing so: 'For if God possesses libertarian freedom, He seems somehow greater and His sovereignty more complete.'[30] I agree with Wainwright about the historical comment. But I think that there is an additional, perhaps stronger, motivation for ascribing libertarian freedom to God than the motive he suggests. If God *necessarily* creates this world and, therefore, cannot avoid creating it, and, in addition, this world necessarily includes us, then it would make no

---

[28] 'Why Only The Best Is Good Enough', *Analysis*, 48 (1988), 224.

[29] 'Jonathan Edwards, William Rowe, and the Necessity of Creation', in Jeff Jordan and Daniel Howard-Snyder (eds.), *Faith, Freedom, and Rationality* (Boston: Roman & Littlefield Publishers, Inc., 1996), 119–33.

[30] Ibid. 128.

for us to thank God or be grateful to God for creating us. Why? use he could not have done anything else but create us. Something in religious attitudes toward God that theistic religions suppose to be proper and right (thanking God for creating us) would not make sense if God lacks libertarian freedom with respect to the world he creates. We would have to give some symbolic interpretation to these religious attitudes, or give them up as senseless, if we came to see that God could not have avoided creating us along with the other items that make up this world. But, as we've seen, this is a controversial matter. For philosophers who deny libertarian freedom to God—Leibniz and Jonathan Edwards, for example—maintain that God is nevertheless responsible for his acts and is justly to be thanked by us and praised for his gracious acts toward us. Despite being controversial, however, theists who are libertarians about freedom cannot avoid this problem.

The main objection Wainwright advances is directed at the fundamental principle that we have employed in our reasoning:

> B. If an omniscient being creates a world when it could have created a better world, then it is possible that there be a being morally better than it.[31]

His objection to Principle B is that it 'obscures the splendor of God's grace'. In developing this objection Wainwright makes three related points about gratuitous love.

(a) gratuitous love is a great good and a highly desirable character trait.

(b) the value of gratuitous love is not a function of the value of the object loved. [We might recall here Robert Adams's account of *grace* as a disposition to love which is not dependent on the merit of the person loved.]

(c) Principle B won't seem compelling to theists who prize gratuitous love and view it as an important element in God's creation of a world.

What shall we say of these three points? Let us agree with both (a) and (b). Where I disagree with Wainwright is his conclusion, registered in (c), that (a) and (b) imply that Principle B is false, or at least doubtful. Wainwright faithfully reports (page 131 of his essay) my objection

---

[31] The way I've stated this principle is slightly different from the version criticized by Wainwright. The difference in no way alters the force of his objection.

(delivered in correspondence with him) to his reasoning. My objection was that we could imagine two omnipotent, omniscient, good beings, G1 and G2, and two worlds, W1 and W2. We can suppose that W2, the world G2 creates, is better than W1, the world G1 creates. And we can suppose that W1's degree of goodness is less than what G2 judges as *acceptable* in a world he is prepared to create, given G2's own degree of goodness; whereas W1's degree of goodness is judged as *acceptable* in a world G1 is prepared to create, given G1's degree of goodness. Further, we can suppose both that G1 creates W1 *because* he gratuitously loves the creatures in W1 and that G2 creates W2 *because* he gratuitously loves the creatures in W2. Doesn't it seem true, nevertheless, that G2 is better than G1? For G2's degree of goodness is such that he is unwilling to create the less good world W1 when he is able to create the better world W2; whereas G1 is prepared to create W1 even though he is able to create the better world G2. In any case, it doesn't seem that the nature and value of gratuitous love can play any role in reaching a negative answer. And, as Wainwright notes, if what we have said works for G1 and G2, we can go on to imagine G3, G4, etc.

Wainwright says that my objection to his claim that Principle B cannot accommodate the importance of gratuitous love in Christian thinking about creation presupposes a further principle.

III. Other things being equal, if an omnipotent and omniscient being, A, is willing to settle for a creatable world which is less good than the world which another omnipotent and omniscient being, B, is willing to settle for, A is less good than B (and hence isn't perfect).

I believe Wainwright is right about Principle III being presupposed in the way I was (when we discussed this matter) putting my objection. I would now put it somewhat differently. In place of III, I would suggest the following principle as being presupposed.

III*. Other things being equal, if an omnipotent, omniscient being's degree of goodness is such that he judges as acceptable for creation a world that is less good than any world which another omnipotent, omniscient being, given its degree of goodness, judges as acceptable for creation, this fact constitutes evidence that the first being is less good than the second (and hence isn't perfect).

Wainwright claims that my response 'doesn't fully accommodate the central role God's gratuitous love plays in *Christian* theism'. Returning to G1 and G2, and noting that there are worlds available for G1 to create that are not available to G2 to create (i.e., the worlds that are judged unacceptable for creation by G2, given his degree of goodness, but still are within the range of worlds judged acceptable for creation by G1, given his degree of goodness), Wainwright proceeds to make two points:

1. G2 has less scope for the exercise of gratuitous love than has G1. (132)
2. 'the less worthy the vessel, the more splendid the grace.' (132)

In an endnote to (1) Wainwright recognizes that if for every creatable world there is a better creatable world, G2 has an infinite number of opportunities to exercise gratuitous love. So what is the objection? 'The fact remains that *more* opportunities are available to [G1].'[32] I don't think it is quite right to say that G1 has more opportunities available to it to exercise gratuitous love than has G2. Quantitatively speaking, G2 has the same number of opportunities available to it as G1 has available to it. It is true that G1 has some poorer opportunities (worlds) in which to exercise its gratuitous love than has G2. But whichever world either selects to create, each will have had an infinite number of yet *better opportunities* to have exercised gratuitous love. So, given that whatever world G2 creates he could have selected from an *infinite* number of better worlds, it is hard to credit a complaint that G2 somehow doesn't have enough scope to exercise his gratuitous love.

I have some difficulty squaring Wainwright's second point ('the less worthy the vessel, the more splendid the grace') with what gratuitous love is supposed to be. Earlier we noted Wainwright's point that 'the value of gratuitous love is not a function of the value of the object loved'. And I noted its resemblance to Robert Adams's account of *grace* as a disposition to love which is not dependent on the merit of the person loved. If Wainwright now says that 'the less worthy the vessel, the more splendid the grace', isn't he implying that the value of gratuitous love is, after all, a function of the value of the object loved? There does seem to be a connection between the worthiness of the vessel and the merit or value of the vessel. Some persons may be more worthy of being loved than other persons. But gratuitous love isn't and cannot be given because of the degree to which a person merits (or fails to merit)

---

[32] Ibid. 304, italics mine.

being loved. If I love A more than B because A is less deserving of being loved than is B, my love is no more *gratuitous* than if I loved B more than A because B is more deserving of love. Gratuitous love is a disposition to love that has nothing to do with the question of how much or how little someone is *worthy* of being loved. It is love without regard to the merit (whatever it may be) of the object loved.

In the second edition of his excellent textbook, *Philosophy of Religion*,[33] Wainwright advances a further interesting objection. In the no best world scenario, his objection is that my argument, based on Principle B, is *illegitimate* because although I fault God for not doing what he could have done (create a better world)—as opposed to faulting him for not doing what logically couldn't be done (create the best possible world)— my complaint is such that it is logically impossible for God to avoid it. For had he created a better world than he did, the same *type* of complaint could be made again, since no matter what world he creates there will be a better world he could have created. Here is what Wainwright says in *Philosophy of Religion*:

Thus, no matter what God did, He would be exposed to the possibility of a complaint of this type. But . . . a type of complaint which is always in place is never in place. A complaint is only legitimate when the person whose conduct is criticized could have acted in such a way that he or she would not be exposed to a complaint of that type. For example, other things being equal, it would be unfair to blame someone for the unfortunate consequences of his or her action if all of the available alternatives would have had equally unfortunate consequences.[34]

What Wainwright says here resembles somewhat the criticism raised by Hasker. But there is a very important difference. Hasker's criticism was that it is a mistake to hold (as I do) that if God creates a world, say W1, then he may be faulted for doing less good than he can. But, as we saw in examining Hasker's criticism, this isn't a mistake. For God would have done better than he did (create W1) had he created, say, world W100. And had he done so, he would not be at fault for creating W1. Wainwright acknowledges this. His point is different. Suppose God had created W100, rather than W1. Then, as I noted in replying to Hasker, he would not be at fault for creating W1. No one can be at fault for something he did not do—not even God! But, I claimed, God would then be at fault for creating W100, given that he could have created a much better world instead, say W1000. But, says Wainwright, this is the

---

[33] *Philosophy of Religion* (2nd edn., Wadsworth, 1999).   [34] Ibid. 92.

same *type* of complaint that would hold for *any world* God might create in the no best world scenario. And Wainwright's point here seems right. Although it is not one and the same complaint, it is the same *type* of complaint. And that established, Wainwright then says, as we noted:

But . . . a type of complaint which is always in place is never in place. A complaint is only legitimate when the person whose conduct is criticized could have acted in such a way that he or she would not be exposed to a complaint of that type.

In examining the criticism advanced by Wainwright, we should note in passing that the example with which he concludes his criticism is not germane to the case at hand. If all the available alternatives—whether finite or infinite in number—have consequences that are the *same in value*, it would not be true that had the person acted differently something better would have resulted. It is surely a mistake to criticize someone for not having done better if there is nothing better that could have been done. But what is involved in the case under scrutiny is the existence of an infinity of *increasingly better creatable worlds* than the one that was selected for creation. If the creator's choice were limited to selecting from an infinity of *equally good worlds*, there would be no basis on which to conclude that the creator's degree of goodness is less than perfect. That is not the case at hand. And I claim that in the case at hand—an infinity of increasingly better worlds—there is a basis on which to conclude that the creator's degree of goodness is less than perfect. Second, and more to the point, we should note that no complaint or criticism is being made of the creator of the world. [I think Wainwright is right in pointing out that a *complaint* against the creator would be inappropriate if *the very same type* of *complaint* could be made no matter what good world he created.] Rather, a *reason* is being given for thinking that the creator's degree of goodness is surpassable. For it would seem to be logically possible for there to be an omnipotent, omniscient being whose degree of goodness is such that, given an infinity of increasingly better worlds than the actual world, he would judge the world that happens to be actual as insufficiently good to be acceptable as a candidate for creation. Of course, given omniscience, omnipotence, and no best world, any creator will know that doing the best that can be done is impossible. But given an infinity of increasingly better worlds from a base starting point of a minimally good world, such a creator presumably will select a world from the range of increasingly better worlds that is *acceptable for creation given the creator's own degree of goodness.* (Theists will not deny that there are minimally good worlds that are less good than the actual world. Presumably they would also be prepared to agree that there are minimally good worlds in that set that were judged unacceptable for creation by the creator of this world, assuming that some omnipotent, omniscient, good being created this world.) But since there is no end to increasingly better worlds, there need be no end to the increasingly greater degrees of goodness in possible creators resulting in increasingly better sets of worlds judged as acceptable for creation. So far as I can see, three assumptions underlie this view. We can express these assumptions as follows:

A1. A good, omnipotent, omniscient being selects a particular world for creation only if he judges that world as acceptable for creation, given his own degree of goodness.

A2. Given an infinity of increasingly good worlds and an omnipotent, omniscient being who creates one of these worlds, it is logically possible that there should be an omnipotent, omniscient being whose degree of goodness is such that he would judge that world, given its degree of goodness, as unacceptable for creation.

A3. The degree of goodness of a world that is acceptable for creation by an omnipotent, omniscient, good being is indicative of the degree of goodness of that being.

Given these assumptions, it is true that if there is an infinity of increasingly good creatable worlds and no best creatable world, then no matter what world an omnipotent, omniscient being creates his degree of goodness is surpassable. But to point this out is not to raise a *complaint* against this being. It is simply to note what follows from the three assumptions just noted. These three assumptions underlie Principle B: If an omniscient being creates a world when there is a better world that it could have created, then it is possible that there exists a being better than it.

The assumption that *appears* to beg the question against the views of Kretzmann, Morris, Hasker, and Wainwright is A3, or perhaps A2 as well. What A3 is meant to imply is that if there is a best creatable world, an omnipotent, omniscient, good being who created a less good world would be less than perfectly good. For in creating less than the best it expresses its own degree of goodness as less than that of an omnipotent, omniscient being whose degree of goodness is such that it would judge as unacceptable for creation any world less than the best. Some theists, perhaps including Kretzmann, Morris, Hasker, and Wainwright, have no difficulty in accepting A3 when it is being supposed that there is a best creatable world. In that case, however, these three assumptions leave little room for libertarian freedom in an omnipotent, omniscient, perfectly good creator. As we've seen, Leibniz and Edwards, operating with assumptions somewhat like these, embrace the conclusion that God creates the best and lacks libertarian freedom. Rather than abandon libertarian freedom with respect to God's selection of a world to create, Kretzmann, Morris, Hasker, and Wainwright opt for the view that there is no best world, finding some support for this view in Aquinas. But now the assumptions that seemed plausible when we were supposing that there is a best world are seen to have an embarrassing result for theism: there is no omnipotent, omniscient, perfectly good creator of a world. Principles that were regarded as plausible on the supposition that there is a best creatable world suddenly become question-begging and inappropriate when we entertain the hypothesis that there is no best creatable world.

Consider the following three propositions:

I. There necessarily exists an essentially omnipotent, essentially omniscient, essentially perfectly good being who has created a world.

II. If an omniscient being creates a world when there is a better world that it could have created, then it is possible that there exists a being morally better than it.

III. For any creatable world there is a better creatable world.

These three propositions form an inconsistent set. Where are we, epistemically speaking, with respect to these three propositions? I suspect we are not all in the same epistemic situation. But what I want to respond to is the charge that in appealing to my Principle B (proposition II) I am begging the question against theism (I). I reject that charge. Of course, if B (i.e., II) is true then, proposition I is false *if* III is true. But I certainly am not supposing that III is true. All I'm *holding* to be true and trying to support is II. Consider, then, two arguments:

Theist's Argument	Non-Theist's Argument
I.	II.
III.	III.
therefore,	therefore,
∼ II.	∼ I.

Each argument is valid and employs the same second premiss. Of course, both I and II could be false, so far as any of us can prove. On the other hand, both I and II could be true (as Leibniz and Edwards most likely believed), in which case the second premiss (III) of both arguments would have to be false—the actual world would be the best creatable world. But we don't know whether III is true or false. And I suspect we have no way of directly proving that III is true or proving that it is false. If we could prove that I and II are true, we could prove that III is false—in which case supporters of Leibniz and Edwards would rejoice. But, in my judgment, we are far from *proving* either I or II. II is a Leibnizian-like principle. Thus, I think it is a mistake to charge that assenting to it is begging the question against theism. To embrace II in the context of supposing that there is a best creatable world, but then to abandon it when confronted with the idea that for every creatable world there is a better is not question-begging either. But it does indicate a resolve to defend I at all costs. Of course, if one is certain that I is true, that may well be the rational thing to do. Perhaps the significance of Principle B can be summed up as follows. If Principle B is true then either (*a*) the actual world is the best creatable world or (*b*) classical theism (as expressed in I) is false.

VI

In a very important contribution to the literature bearing on the topic of the problem of no best world,[35] Bruce Langtry argues that our seemingly plausible principle

> B. *if an omniscient being creates a world when there is a better world it could create, then it would be possible for there to be a being morally better than it*

is in fact false. In understanding his view it is important to note that although he takes God to be *essentially* all-powerful, all-knowing, and perfectly good, he does not assume that if God exists he *necessarily* exists. It is also to be noted that when writing about a world, Langtry understands a *world* in the sense introduced in Chapter 5, where a possible world just is a maximal state of affairs.[36] And for our purposes we may

---

[35] 'God and the Best', *Faith and Philosophy* (July 1996) 311–28. Page references appear in the text.

[36] As we saw, a state of affairs S is maximal if for every state of affairs S′, S includes S′ or S precludes S′.

suppose that for God to create a possible world is just for God to bring it about that some possible world is *actual*, or, as Langtry would say, it is for God to *instantiate* some possible world (maximal state of affairs).

Taking a *prime* world to be a world such that God (if he exists) can actualize it and cannot actualize a better world than it, Langtry, without much in the way of argument, suggests that we don't (or can't) *know* whether, if God exists, there are any *prime* worlds. And, of course, if we can't know whether God's being a world creator requires the existence of a prime world, then, as far as we know, God could exist and create a world even though there is an infinity of increasingly better worlds any of which he supposedly could have created instead. So, if Langtry is right and we cannot know that God's being a world creator requires the existence of a prime world, then we cannot know that Principle B is true.

Surprisingly, there is much in Langtry's reasoning that comes close to the view we've been supporting. For example, he endorses the principle:

Other things being equal, in intentionally bringing about the better state of affairs one acts in the morally better way. (322)

And after considering several defeaters relevant to this principle so far as human behavior is concerned, he concludes that none apply with respect to God's choosing not to create a prime world. Indeed, at one point he explicitly states:

A being who could have acted in a morally better way is not morally perfect. (323)

And, as we have seen, any being who creates a world when it could have created a better world certainly could have acted in a morally better way than it did. But, perhaps sensing the apparent problem, Langtry follows the sentence quoted above [Other things being equal, in intentionally bringing about the better state of affairs one acts in the morally better way.] with the statement:

This principle can easily be misunderstood. It does not entail that if there are no prime worlds then God is not perfectly good. (323)

Of course, what Langtry says here is technically correct. Since we both agree that God's nature includes perfect goodness it is impossible for God to exist and be other than perfectly good. The issue isn't whether the principle

Other things being equal, in intentionally bringing about the better state of affairs one acts in the morally better way entails that God isn't perfectly good. The issue is whether it entails that no existing being that acts in a certain way when it could have acted in a morally better way (other things being equal) can be God.

It is also clear in Langtry's view

that there is no pair of worlds, V and W, such that God's actualizing V is a morally better action than God's actualizing W, even though W remains the better world. (325)

As we've seen, then, there is much in Langtry's essay that is compatible with our principle:

if an omniscient being creates a world when there is a better world it could create, then it would be possible for there to be a being morally better than it.

But it is also clear that he thinks this principle (Principle B) is false. In a lengthy endnote (327) Langtry quotes the relevant passage from my essay, 'The Problem of Divine Perfection and Freedom'. Here is that quotation:

A being is necessarily an absolutely perfect being only if it is not possible for there to be a being morally better than it. If a being creates a world when there is some morally better world that it could have created, then it is possible that there be a being better than it. . . . [Therefore] the existence of the theistic God who creates a world is inconsistent with the supposition that among the worlds he can create there is no morally unsurpassable world.

Stating that he disagrees with my second premiss [If a being creates a world when there is some morally better world that it could have created, then it is possible that there be a being better than it], Langtry explains why.

We ought, in the present context, be discontent with any mere appeal to intuition in defense of Rowe's premise, but rather demand an argument in favor of it. The strongest argument I can think of appeals to my premise (4), from Section 5: other things being equal, in intentionally bringing about the better state of affairs one acts in the morally better way. But *when a being is choosing a world to create from an infinite hierarchy of better and better worlds*, the conclusion that one could always have acted in a morally better way is defeated by the fact that some worlds are *good enough*. Rejection of what would be entirely acceptable were it not for the option of choosing the better would be no sign of superior excellence of character; rather the defective nature of the attitude would be shown in the paralysis and self-stultification which it induced. (327)

I assume from what he says that Langtry sees that intuition tends to support Principle B—thus his remark that we should not rest on intuition here but ask *in addition* for some *argument* in favor of Principle B. And as I stated earlier, I do think that Principle B is strongly supported by our intuitive sense. In fact, where the series of increasingly better worlds is finite (culminating in a *prime* world), rather than infinite, Principle B gives the result Langtry endorses—God's creating a *prime* world. Indeed, I think that the intuitive appeal of Principle B is sufficient to carry the day, barring an effective objection to Principle B. So, what is Langtry's objection?

Langtry acknowledges, of course, that in the no best creatable world scenario the creator will always be subject to the objection that *he could have acted in a morally better way.* And this is so no matter what he does or does not do. If he creates no world at all, he will have failed to do what is better (creating a good world) than not creating at all. If he creates a particular good world, he will have failed to do what is better than creating the world he did. For he will have failed to create an even better world, instead of the world he created. But this conclusion (*in the no best world scenario*)—that he could have acted in a morally better way—is, claims Langtry, defeated by the fact that some worlds are *good enough.*

What Langtry seems to be saying here is that as we consider an unending series of worlds ordered in terms of increasing goodness, there will be a point at which we will reach a world whose degree of goodness is such that it is *perfectly acceptable* for creation by God, even if there is a better world that God could create instead of creating it—for it possesses that degree of goodness that is *good enough* for God to create it, regardless of whether or not there are other creatable worlds whose degree of goodness exceeds, even greatly exceeds, its degree of goodness. But a moment's reflection suffices to show that this cannot be what he means. For no matter how good a world may be, Langtry holds that if it is a world in a series of worlds culminating in a *prime* world—a world God can actualize and cannot actualize a better world than it—then God, if he creates at all, must create the prime world. No world less than the prime world is good enough for God to create. And this being so, Langtry's view cannot but strike us as somewhat paradoxical. For suppose that God is confronting an *infinite* series of increasingly better worlds: W1, W2, W3, etc., etc. There simply is no best world for God to actualize. Following Langtry's principle, seeing that there is no best world to create, God then examines each of the worlds and sees, let us say, that unlike W1 or W2, W3 has that degree of goodness that is 'good enough' and proceeds to actualize it even though there is an infinity of increasingly better worlds any one of which God could have selected instead as the world to actualize. This makes it seem that being 'good enough' is an intrinsic property of W3, a property that it has no matter what, just as 'being good' is an intrinsic property of happiness and love; whereas 'being bad' is an intrinsic property of unhappiness and hate. But this can't be what Langtry means to imply. For suppose instead that W3 were a member of a series of increasingly better worlds that terminates in a best creatable world. If so, then W3 does not possess the property of being 'good enough' for God to create it. Indeed, no world in the series of increasingly better worlds—other than the prime world terminating the series—has that property. So, it depends on something other than the intrinsic merit of W3 as to whether it is 'good enough' for God to create.

Langtry's view comes down to this. Consider an *infinite* series of increasingly better creatable worlds. We can refer to this series of increasingly better worlds as the series: W1, W2, W3, etc., etc. If God is confronted with this infinite series of increasingly better creatable worlds, it is obvious that he cannot do his *best* in creating. For any world he creates it will be true that he could have created a better world, that in creating the world he selects he does *less good* than he is able to do. Does that make it morally alright for God to create the *least good* world, W1? Surely not. A being who purposely creates the least good world of an infinite series of increasingly better worlds (any one of which he could have created instead) can hardly portray himself as an unsurpassably good creator. For W1, as Langtry would (should) undoubtedly say, is simply 'not good enough' for God to create given that he can instead create any world in the infinite series of increasingly better worlds. What then of W10, or perhaps W100? Would a being who purposely chose to create W100, when he could have created instead a world that is a billion times better than W100, be an *absolutely perfect being*, a being than which a *better creator* is not even *possible*? Again, it seems clear that there could be a being whose degree of *goodness* is such that he simply would not choose to create W100 when he could instead create a world that is a billion times better than W100. It's clear, that is, that in creating W1, W10, or W100 from among an infinite array of increasingly better creatable worlds, an infinitely powerful creator would be doing less good that he can, and therefore would not be an *absolutely perfect being*. Indeed, no matter what world an infinitely powerful creator would select, it is possible that there should be another world creator whose degree of *goodness* would preclude it from creating that world, given that it is able instead to create any of an infinite series of increasingly better worlds.

But Langtry denies all this, holding instead that:

Rejection of what would be entirely acceptable were it not for the option of choosing the better would be no sign of superior excellence of character.

He advances this principle as though it is *obvious* just what worlds are entirely acceptable for creation—apart from there being a better world that one could choose to create instead. But so far as one can tell from what he says, Langtry must think that even if there is an infinity of increasingly better creatable worlds, W1, W2, W3, etc., etc., a being who is able to create any one of the worlds in this series could create the minimally good world, W1, and still be *the world creator than which no morally better world creator is possible.* For, I daresay, if the *only* creatable good world were W1, the world creator than which no morally better world creator is possible would be justified in creating it. For the alternative is not to create a world at all—given that a morally good creator would certainly *not* create a world that is not a good world. And creating a minimally good world may well be better than not creating at all. But if that is so, then what Langtry is telling us is that God would be fully justified in creating the *least good of an infinite series of increasing better creatable worlds, any one of which he could have chosen instead of the least good world.*

Suppose on approaching your grocery store at Christmas time you see the familiar Salvation Army pot for contributions to the poor. You have just won the lottery and are carrying many thousands of dollars in bills in your briefcase. On inspecting the briefcase crammed with bills, you realize that you have in your possession every denomination from a one dollar bill to a one hundred dollar bill, many times over. Knowing that giving any sum of money is better than not giving at all, you decide to contribute to the Salvation Army. And given your present enormous wealth, you realize that with no hardship at all to yourself you can give a bill of any denomination from a one dollar bill to a one hundred dollar bill. (Not wanting to appear ostentatious, you only consider giving a single bill from among the thousands of bills in your possession.) Despite your sure knowledge of the greater good that would result from your giving a larger bill, you nevertheless select the smallest bill in your possession, a one dollar bill, to contribute. What do you here show yourself to be? Whatever it is, it is surely not 'a giver (of a single bill) to the Salvation Army than which a more generous giver (of a single bill) is not possible'. And would it change matters if we were to imagine the sum of money in your possession to be double (triple, quadruple, quintuple, etc., etc.) the amount it actually is? No. In fact the more money you have in your possession, even were it somehow an *infinite amount*, would only make matters worse were you still to give just one dollar.

Well, how is it different with a world creator? Clearly, in many important ways. The world creator is selecting, we will suppose, among an infinite number of possible worlds. And he is selecting exactly one to make actual. But these possible worlds, let us suppose, differ in degrees of goodness. Presumably, given that he is a good world creator, if there are any worlds that are overall bad he will not choose to actualize any of them. Some possible worlds are on the whole good, but contain a fair number of creatures who suffer needlessly. Other possible worlds are much better overall. And, let us suppose there is a world better than all the rest, a *best of all creatable worlds*. Isn't it evident that were this world creator to pass over the very best world and deliberately actualize a minimally good world, a world containing, say, a considerable amount of unjustified suffering, he would show himself to be something *less* than a *morally perfect* creator? I take it that the answer is obvious. And it doesn't make it any better for our world creator if we try to suppose that he selects that world knowing that there is an infinity of increasingly better worlds any one of which he could have chosen instead. For in the no best world scenario no matter what world a creator creates he will fail to do as good as he can. And, as we've seen, what this shows is that although it is possible that there be a world creator than which a better world creator is not possible and also possible that there be no best creatable world, these two possibilities are not jointly possible.

VII

In their essay, 'Must God Create?',[37] Sandra Menssen and Thomas Sullivan argue that God created with absolute freedom. And by *God's absolute freedom in creating* they understand both that God was free not to create at all, and that God was free to create some world other than the

---

[37] 'Must God Create?', *Faith and Philosophy* (July 1995), 321–41. Further references appear in the text.

world he did create. Both sorts of freedom, they tell us, are supported by what is said in the scriptures, as well as by such seminal figures in the history of the Church as Augustine and Aquinas. Moreover, they note that in the nineteenth century:

Vatican I recognized the Church's constant teaching concerning God's free creation as defined dogma: it is an article of faith for Catholics that God created 'by a volition free from all necessity'. (321)

In their essay they propose to defend God's *absolute freedom* in creation against two theistic arguments, the first based on Leibniz's 'proof' that God must create the best possible world, and the second based on the Dionysian principle that goodness is essentially diffusive of itself, a principle taken by some to imply the necessity of God's creating some world or other. Along the way they also consider several other lines of argument, including Philip Quinn's principle to the effect that if a being does less than the best it can do, it is possible that there be a being better than it.

Taking it as given that God exists, our authors are not inclined to disagree with the principle:

Where possible world x is better than possible world y, God's act of creating x will be better that his act of creating y. (325)

What they do disagree with is the principle:

If one action is better than another, then God cannot choose the less perfect action over the more perfect action. (327)

Why do they reject this seemingly plausible principle? Here is their argument.

Suppose there is no best possible world. Then God must choose a state of affairs less good than another he could have chosen, whatever he does (this is assuming that creating nothing is choosing a state of affairs). (327)

But if (no matter what he does) God must choose a state of affairs less good than another he could have chosen, then it is obviously senseless to suppose the principle in question: that God cannot choose the less perfect action over the more perfect action. For there is no way he can avoid doing so. [We may observe in passing that in arguing as they do our authors are simply assuming, with no argument at all, that Principle B (*If an omniscient being creates a world when there is a better world it could create, then it would be possible for there to be a being morally better than it*) is false. For if Principle B is true then, of course, it cannot be true both that

God creates a world and there is no best creatable world. For then it would be possible that the best possible being is a being than which a better being is possible.]

Our authors also profess that it seems to them to be 'completely arbitrary' both to *require* that God create a material world, 'to hold that God's creation is necessary', but *allow* that God might create some world less good than another he could create instead. So, they conclude that since it is possible that God create a world less good than another, it is also possible that God not create at all.

It must be admitted, I believe, that this last argument is not very compelling. If we suppose that it is better for God to create a good world than not to create a world at all, the fact that there is no best world for God to create hardly makes it unnecessary for God to create some good world. If there is a problem, as I think there is, with there being no best world for God to create, the problem isn't that it makes it unnecessary for God to create a good world. The problem is that it makes it impossible for God to do as good as he can, and thereby makes it possible for there to be a world creator who is better than God.

But let's consider more carefully their argument to prove the falsity of the following principle (their principle 2c):

> *if one action is better than another, then God cannot choose the less perfect action over the more perfect action.*

They start by supposing, of course, that God exists. They also suppose that for God to create nothing (not create at all) is for God to *choose* a state of affairs (presumably the state of affairs: God's not creating something). Suppose then, our authors say, 'there is no best possible world'. What follows, of course, is that 'God must choose a state of affairs less good than he could have chosen.' But if, whatever he chooses, God chooses some state of affairs less good than another he could have chosen instead, 'why would one stipulate that the action he chooses to perform must be better than one of the (good) choices he could have made, which consists of not creating any material world?' (327).

The argument here amounts to this. We are supposing that God is confronted with an infinite number of different choices. Each of these choices, save the first, consists in his creating a world. The second choice is to create a minimally good world, W1. The third choice is to create a slightly better world, W2. The fourth choice is to create a world (W3) that is slightly better than W2, etc., etc. The first choice is simply the choice not to create any world at all, even the least good world, W1. And we will suppose with our authors that the first choice is not a bad choice, although it is not clear from anything they say that there is any reason to believe that it itself is a good choice. But whether that be so or not, it is clear both that the choice to create Wn is a better choice than the choice to create Wn−1, and, therefore, so it seems, that the choice to create W1 is a better choice than the choice to create no world at all.

With this background we can now evaluate the argument our authors have given to disprove the principle: *if one action is better than another, then God cannot choose the less perfect action over the more perfect action.* In their argument our authors simply *assume* that it is possible for God to be in a situation where he cannot avoid performing an action less good than some other action he could perform instead. For they assume God to be in a situation in which there is an infinity of increasingly better acts of world creation, any one of which he can perform, and that in choosing not to create a world he thereby performs *the act* of not creating any world at all. So, the situation they describe has built into it the *absolute necessity* of God's performing an action when he could have performed an action better than it.

But why should we *assume*, as our authors do, that it is *possible* for God to perform an action that is less good than some other action he could perform instead? Why should we assume that it is *possible* for God to be forced to submit to a situation in which his desire to do what is best is frustrated? In short, why should we assume, as our authors do, that it is possible both for God to exist and for there to be no best world? Our authors give no reason at all for making this assumption. They do see, however, that if one does make this assumption, one cannot also accept the seemingly plausible thesis: If one action is better than another (all things considered), a perfect being would not choose to perform the less good action rather than the (all things considered) better action.

Consider the propositions:

(1) God exists and creates a world.

(2) There is no best creatable world.

(3) If one action is better than another, God cannot choose to perform the less perfect action over the more perfect action.

Our authors see (correctly, in my judgment) that, taken together, these three propositions imply a contradiction.[38] So, one of them, at least, must be false. A follower of Leibniz will accept (1) and (3), and reject (2) as false.

---

[38] In order to simplify their argument I here assume that: necessarily, if x is a better world than y then creating x is a better 'action' than creating y or creating nothing.

Our authors, of course, accept (1) as true. So, they must reject either (2) or (3). What about (2)? Well, to reject (2) as false leaves one with a dilemma: to explain how it can be that the actual world is the *best* creatable world; or to explain how it can be that God has chosen to create a world less than the best when he could have chosen to create the very best world. Defending either horn of this dilemma is a task whose prospects for success are doubtful at best. So, our authors, not unwisely, choose instead to argue that (3) is false. What, then, is their argument to show that (3) is in fact false? It is their answer to this question that simply begs the question at issue among those who may disagree about which of (1), (2), and (3) is to be rejected. For, as we noted earlier, the totality of their argument for the falsity of (3) is this:

Suppose there is no best possible world. Then God must choose a state of affairs less good than another he could have chosen, whatever he does (this is assuming that creating nothing is choosing a state of affairs). (327)

In short, their argument for the falsity of (3) is that one of (1), (2), and (3) must be false, and both (1) and (2) are true. But since the central question at issue is which of (1), (2), and (3) is false, or which is it more reasonable to reject as false, it simply begs the question at issue to say, in effect, that (3) is false because (1) and (2) are true. What our authors need to do is to give an independent, compelling argument for the conclusion that it is *possible* for an essentially perfect being intentionally to choose to perform an action that is less good (all things considered) than some other action he can perform instead. As it stands, they simply assume, without argument, that it is possible.

VIII

In his article, 'The Freedom of God',[39] Edward Wierenga advances several important objections to the fundamental principle (Principle B) that I have been supporting and using to show that the classical conception of God as a necessarily existing, essentially omniscient, omnipotent, perfectly good being who freely creates a world is *inconsistent* with the claim that there is no best creatable world. Wierenga begins by noting that since God is essentially omniscient, omnipotent, and perfectly good, it appears to follow that 'whenever God is in circumstances C in which a

---

[39] 'The Freedom of God', *Faith and Philosophy* (Oct. 2002), 425–36. Further references appear in the text.

certain action A is the best action, he would know that A is the best action, he would want to do A, and he would be able to do A' (425). But, then, it also seems to be true that 'If in C God knows that A is the best action, wants to do A, and is able to do A, then God does A in C' (426). In fact, as Wierenga observes, this last proposition 'would seem to be a necessary truth—how could an omnibenevolent, omnipotent, and omniscient God fail to do what he knew to be best, wanted to do, and was able to do?' (426). Wierenga then notes the problem for divine freedom:

if God is ever in such circumstances, it would seem that he is unable in those circumstances to refrain from performing the action in question. He could not refrain from performing the action in those circumstances, since it is impossible that he be in those circumstances and not perform it. (426)

But then, of course, on the *libertarian* conception of freedom God does not freely perform that action in those circumstances. Wierenga cites with favor Thomas Flint's characterization of libertarian freedom: 'an agent is truly free with respect to an action only if the situation in which he is placed is logically and causally compatible with both his performing and his not performing the action.'[40] And he notes that both Thomas Flint and Richard Swinburne appear to agree with the view he has set forth, that, as Swinburne says: 'God's perfect goodness . . . constrains him to act in certain ways.'[41] Indeed, Swinburne accepts the view that 'if there is a best action, [God] will do it', adding that 'if there are alternative equal best actions, he will do one of them'.[42]

Thus far, it would appear that Swinburne and Flint, as well Wierenga, agree with me concerning the *necessity* of God's always doing (and therefore, not *freely* doing) what he sees to be the best course of action. So, clearly, if there is a best action for God to perform (e.g., creating the best world), God creates the best world of necessity, not freely. And just as clearly, if there are alternative best worlds for God to perform, he will of necessity, not freely, create one of them—although the *particular* one he selects may be freely chosen from among the set of equally good creatable worlds.[43] Thus far there is substantial agreement between the view I support and the view endorsed by Flint, Swinburne, and Wier-

[40] Thomas P. Flint, 'The Problem of Divine Freedom', *American Philosophical Quarterly*, 20 (1983), 255–264, at 255.

[41] Richard Swinburne, *The Christian God* (Oxford: Clarendon Press, 1994), 134.

[42] Ibid. 135.

[43] Even though there being several creatable worlds than which there are none better appears to leave God *free* to create any one of these worlds, Swinburne and other proponents

enga. The trouble begins when we consider the 'possibility' of there being an infinite series or range of increasingly better choices open to God, only one of which can be selected. Wierenga cites the following passage from Swinburne.

often the range of actions open to God is an infinite range of actions, each of which is inferior to some other action. Thus, for any world of conscious agents which God could create *ex nihilo*, there is plausibly a better one—for instance, one obtained by adding one more conscious agent (sufficiently distant from the others not to crowd them). And so among the actions of creating conscious agents *ex nihilo* there is no best.[44]

Presumably, when Swinburne says 'there is *plausibly* a better one' he means to suggest that the added conscious agent contributes to the world being better, rather than being someone whose acts result in the world of conscious agents being less good than it would be without him. In any case, here is Wierenga's gloss on the Swinburne remark just cited.

In Swinburne's example, if it is better to have a world with conscious agents created *ex nihilo* than not to, then God's goodness constrains him to pick from the infinite range of worlds like that. But the particular choice of alternative, both in the case of ties for best and in the case of infinite series with no best, is up to God. As Swinburne puts it, 'Insofar as he acts within that framework, his perfect goodness does not dictate what he will do; and any acts within that framework we may call acts of will.'[45]

And after noting that Flint's position on the infinity of better acts is similar to Swinburne's, Wierenga concludes: 'So both Swinburne and Flint think that God is free in at least certain situations, namely, when he faces a tie for best alternative or when there is an infinite series of increasingly better alternatives with no best.'[46]

At this point in his lucid discussion of the problem of divine freedom, Wierenga notes that the position embraced by himself, Flint, and Swinburne is in conflict both with the principle advanced by Quinn and the similar principle advanced by me [Principle B: If an omniscient being creates a world when there is a better world it could create, then it would be possible for there to be a being morally better than it]. After reviewing the interchange between me and the Howard-Snyders, Wierenga focuses

of this view are still burdened with having to defend the rather implausible claim that the actual world with all its evil is a world than which it is logically impossible that there should be a better world than it.

[44] Ibid. 41.   [45] 'The Freedom of God', 430.   [46] Ibid.

on Principle B, suggesting that 'Whatever plausibility this principle might have in the case of choices among a finite number of alternatives seems to me to disappear when the choice in question is from among an infinite number of choices where it is better to pick one rather than none.'[47] Of course, it was my aim in the discussion with the Howard-Snyders to show that even if it is better to create a world than to not create at all, in the case of an infinite number of increasingly better worlds, no omnipotent, omniscient being who creates a world could be *supremely perfect*. For no matter what world such a being chooses to create it would be possible for there to be a being whose degree of goodness is such that it simply would not create *that world* given that there is a better world it can create instead. Imagine, for example, that an omniscient, omnipotent deity who is considering an infinite array of increasingly better worlds purposely chooses to create the *least good* world, when it could just as easily have elected to create a world enormously better than it. Would such a being merit the appellation: the world creator than which no *better* world creator is possible? Surely not. But for any world this being might select, he will succeed in doing less good than he can—for there will be an infinite number of better worlds any one of which he could have selected instead. Thus, no matter what world this being selects it will be possible for there to be a being whose degree of goodness is such that he would not choose *that world* to create given that there is a world immensely better than it which he could have chosen instead.

It is unclear to me whether Wierenga thinks my argument fails to carry the day against the Howard-Snyder's vision of an infinite number of increasingly better worlds beginning with a minimally good world, a world than which no lessor world would be acceptable for creation. Wierenga may think that the Howard-Synders' argument is sound but just unconvincing or insufficiently persuasive owing to their supposing that there is a least good world or, as Wierenga puts it, 'a minimal permissible world'. In any case, Wierenga thinks that he can provide a sound argument against Principle B by simply supposing that there is no *least good* creatable world, that for every good creatable world there is a good but less good creatable world. In short, just as there could be no best creatable world, Wierenga thinks there need be no least good creatable world, that for any good creatable world there is a less good creatable world.

---

[47] 'The Freedom of God', 431.

Acknowledging that it is plausible to suppose there could be an infinite series of increasingly better creatable worlds, Wierenga asserts that

it seems equally plausible that there might be no lowest acceptable level of knowledge and power, no shortest acceptable life span, no minimal acceptable amount of pleasure or compensation for evil for a world to be permissible. (432)

His idea here is that just as there might be no best of all possible worlds, there might also be no least good possible world, no minimally good possible world. Suppose, then, that there is no least good world.

In that case, it is hard to see how Thor (who picks a better world than Jove) in the example (the Howard-Snyders give) could be acting on a nobler principle or higher standard than Jove. Each picks a world to which infinitely many worlds are superior and which is itself superior to infinitely many other worlds. Thor does not have a principle according to which he rejects as unsuitable more worlds than Jove rejects. There can be no basis for Thor's rejection of worlds lower than 800, if there are infinitely many in that category; both make an arbitrary choice. These deities can create worlds of differing value without thereby differing themselves in goodness. (432)

The idea Wierenga here appeals to is that if there not only is no best world, but also no least good world, then no matter what world a deity (Thor, Jove) selects for creation there will be an infinite number of increasingly good worlds (ranked above the world he selected) and an infinite number of decreasingly good worlds (ranked below the world he selected). That seems right. But it should be observed that there is an important difference between the two infinite series, the one proceeding upward to increasingly better worlds, and the other proceeding downward to decreasingly good worlds. In the series of increasingly better worlds (the upward series) each world logically could be better than a world below it by the *same degree or amount*. So, for example, if we follow Swinburne, as Wierenga does, for each world there may be a better world than it by virtue of possessing one more creature who enjoys a very good life. And this degree of improvement can be *constant* as we proceed upward in the unending series of increasingly good worlds. It can be constant because there need be no upper limit to this series of increasingly good worlds. But the downward series of decreasingly good worlds does have a lower limit, a world that is not good, or a world that is overall bad. And this means that to prevent reaching a least good world, the downward series cannot be continuously diminished by the same amount of good. Instead, if the degree of good of a particular world is diminished by a certain amount of good (however little you please) to reach the world just below it in the downward series, one must at some point decrease that amount and continue to do so as one proceeds downward, otherwise one will all too soon reach a world that is not good at all. You can start at 100 and add 1 to it continuously without ever running out of positive whole numbers. But you cannot start from 100 (or any particular whole number) and subtract 1 from it continuously without running out of positive whole numbers. You can, however, subtract 1 until you reach a world with 1 degree of good, and then subtract $\frac{1}{2}$, $\frac{1}{4}$, $\frac{1}{8}$, $\frac{1}{16}$, $\frac{1}{32}$, etc., etc., without ever reaching a world of zero degree of good. But short of some such procedure, one cannot start with a world containing a certain finite amount of good and also have an absolutely infinite series of decreasingly good worlds; whereas one can start with a world containing a certain finite amount of good and also have an absolutely infinite series of increasingly good worlds, each better than the one just below it by the same definite amount of good.

The importance of the point just made is that in the downward series of decreasingly good worlds that continually approach but never reach a world with zero degree of good, the difference between one world and the next will eventually be so minimal as to make no *detectable, felt difference* to any sentient being. Creatures are capable of distinguishing degrees of pleasure and pain, but there are mathematical differences in the amount of pleasure or pain that make absolutely no *appreciable, felt difference to the creature.* And any difference between one degree of pleasure and a lessor degree of pleasure that makes absolutely no detectable, appreciable difference to any sentient creature will fail to result in one world being less good or more good than the other. So, the infinite downward series of decreasingly good worlds envisaged by Wierenga is in fact a *finite series* when measured in terms of felt or experienced pleasure or happiness. And a similar point will hold for other forms of experienced goods in the lives of sentient creatures. I conclude, therefore, that the infinite series of decreasingly good worlds envisaged by Wierenga is inapplicable to the topic of good experienced by creatures, and, therefore, ineffective as a response to the problem we've posed.

But let's return to the problem that Wierenga proposes to solve by noting that the series of good worlds need not be construed as beginning with the least good world W1, and proceeding infinitely upward with increasingly better creatable worlds W2, W3, W4, etc., etc. On this model of creatable worlds—where there is a least good world W1—I suggested that Thor, in choosing to refrain from creating from within a certain set of good worlds when he can create a better world, exhibits a higher standard than does Jove who is prepared to create any of the good worlds, including the least good world. I described the difference between them as follows.

Jove and Thor may act on the following principles:

P1. Do not create any world that is not a good world.

P2. Do not create any good world whose goodness is less than what one judges as *acceptable*, given that one can create a better world.

Clearly, both Thor and Jove act in accordance with P1 and P2. Neither is prepared to create a less than good world. And neither is prepared to create a good world whose degree of goodness is less than what he judges as acceptable in a world, given that he can create a better world. The difference between them is this. Jove's standard of goodness in world creating is such that he is prepared to settle for *any* good world even if there is a better that he can create. Thor, however, has a higher standard. He is not prepared to create any of the good worlds from W1 to W800 provided there is a better world that he can create. Of course, Thor's allegiance to P2 does not preclude him absolutely from creating, say, W777. It prevents him only on the condition that there is a better world he can create.

Wierenga, as we saw, does not explicitly reject the reasons I gave (against the contention of the Howard-Snyders) for holding that Thor acts on a higher principle of world-creating than does Jove. Instead, he suggests that the difference I've alleged to hold between Thor and Jove disappears once we suppose that there is no first member of the series of good creatable worlds. For, whereas before (supposing there is a first member of the series of good creatable worlds) Jove rejects a smaller number of worlds than does Thor, thus providing a reason why Thor acts on a higher principle of world-creating than does Jove, now there is no numerical difference between the number of worlds each rejects as suitable for creation. For if there is no least good world, each rejects an infinite number of worlds. And by virtue of this point Wierenga thinks it follows that there is no basis at all for holding that Thor has a higher standard of world-creating than does Jove. Thus he writes:

Each [Jove, Thor] picks a world to which infinitely many worlds are superior and which is itself superior to infinitely many other worlds. Thor does not have a principle according to which he rejects as unsuitable more worlds than Jove rejects. There can be no basis for Thor's rejection of worlds lower than 800, if there are infinitely many in that category; both make an arbitrary choice. These deities can create worlds of differing value without thereby differing themselves in goodness. (432)

Let's consider the last sentence of Wierenga's comment. I agree with him that these deities (Jove, Thor) 'can' create worlds of differing value without thereby differing themselves in goodness. And that can happen even if there is a least good world. After all, they might not care enough about the degree of goodness of the world they each create, for they may not themselves be perfectly good beings. It is important here to remember that the principle in question, Principle B, doesn't say that if a being creates a world when it could have created a better world, then there is a morally better being than it. All it says is that it is *possible* for there to be a being morally better than it. So, when Wierenga argues that deities '*can* create worlds of differing value without thereby differing themselves in goodness', he is not countering anything asserted by Principle B. What Principle B implies with respect to deities who create worlds of differing value is that it is *possible* that the one who creates the world of greater value is morally better than the one creating the world of lessor value. For it is possible that he has a higher standard of world creation such that he will not choose to create the lessor world given that he can create the better world instead.

I don't think that the mistake just noted is a sufficient to answer to Wierenga's basic objection. For his basic objection doesn't rest on that mistake. Rather, his objection rests on the following principle: if two world creators reject the same number of lessor good worlds before choosing the world they are prepared to create, we have no reason to think that one of these beings has a higher standard of world-creating than the other. And given that there is a *least good world* beginning the series of good, creatable worlds, such a principle appears to be entirely reasonable. Thus if they both reject the first 1000 worlds as 'not good enough', and are both prepared to create any world above the first 1000 worlds, then even if they use a random selection machine to pick among the worlds 1001, 1002, 1003, etc., etc., the result will provide no reason to think that the one creator is a morally better creator than the other.

It is with this insight in mind that Wierenga asks us to consider the case in which there is *no least good world*. On this assumption whatever world a creator selects (for creation) will be better than an infinite number of lessor good worlds. Suppose then that in the no best world scenario two world creators select (or would select) different worlds as acceptable for creation. Creator A, say, selects a world that is not as good as the world selected by creator B. Indeed, Wierenga will allow that creator B, unlike creator A, may reject the world selected by A as simply not good enough for B to create, given that there is a better world B can create. So, we have two possible selections for world creation, Wa (the world creator A selects) and Wb (the better world creator B selects). And I suppose that Wierenga will allow that B may decline to create Wa so long as there is a better world he can select instead. But, let us suppose, A is prepared to create Wa even though there is a better world he can select instead. Moreover, let us suppose that A and B each realize that no matter what world he might choose to create, there is a still better world he could have selected instead. Why then do I say that we have reason to think B is a better world creator than A? After all, as Wierenga notes:

Each picks a world to which infinitely many worlds are superior and which is itself superior to infinitely many other worlds. Thor does not have a principle according to which he rejects as unsuitable more worlds than Jove rejects. There can be no basis for Thor's rejection of worlds lower than 800, if there are infinitely many in that category; both make an arbitrary choice. (432)

It is worth noting that even though both reject infinitely many worlds as unsuitable for creation, given that one can create a better world, Thor rejects *all* the worlds that Jove rejects, but in addition rejects some worlds that Jove considers as acceptable. Shouldn't this point show that Thor has a higher standard of world creation than Jove? 'No,' replies Wierenga, for 'if there are infinitely many in that category; both make an arbitrary choice' (432).

Wierenga is claiming, I believe, that it makes sense to think that Thor (who chooses to create a world that is better than the world Jove chooses to create) has a higher standard of world creation than Jove *only if* Thor rejects a *larger number* of worlds than is rejected by Jove. Apparently, it is not enough for Wierenga that Thor's standard for world creation requires him to reject not only *all* the worlds (an infinite number) that Jove rejects, but also some worlds that Jove finds acceptable, including the world that Jove elects to create. And Thor rejects those worlds, we may suppose, because his own standard of world creation is such that he judges those worlds to be not good enough for him to create, provided he can create a better world. My own best judgment is that Wierenga has failed to show that it *makes no sense* in the 'no least good world scenario' to suppose that Jove acts on a higher standard of world creation than does Thor. For it remains true that Thor elects to create a *better world* than the world Jove elects to create, and true also that Thor chooses that world over the world chosen by Jove *because* it is a better world.

Despite his efforts to defend the view of Swinburne and Flint that an infinite series of increasingly better worlds leaves God free to create any world in that series, in the end Wierenga argues that their view leaves God insufficiently free. For in Wierenga's judgment the view endorsed by Swinburne and Flint 'amounts to saying that God is free only *when it does not matter what he does*' (432).

In any situation in which there is a best action open to God, Swinburne and Flint agree that his nature compels him to do it. They only find room for God's freedom in circumstances in which any choice he makes is on a par with any other, where he might as well choose blindly or randomly, and that is not a significant amount of freedom. (433)

What, then, is Wierenga's proposal to enlarge the scope of God's freedom? Wierenga begins by noting the two different conditions that on the view of Swinburne and Flint preclude an agent from acting freely: antecedent conditions that render it *causally impossible* for the agent to do or will otherwise, and antecedent conditions that render it *logically impossible* for the agent to do otherwise. Compatibilists (those who hold that causal determinism does not preclude free actions) distinguish between causal determinants such as our beliefs and desires and causal determinants that are external to us or internal but forced on us, holding that being determined by our naturally formed beliefs and desires is consistent with freedom and responsibility for the outputs of such beliefs and desires. (Never mind that those beliefs and desires are the inevitable result of a causal chain of events proceeding from the distant past.) Following the lead of such compatibilists, Wierenga proposes the following:

Let us apply the compatibilist's insight to the case of God. Even if in some circumstances C God's knowing that A is the best action, his wanting to do A, and his being able to do A is a logically sufficient condition of his doing A in C, it is nevertheless in virtue of *his own nature* that he knows that A is the best action, wants to do A, and is able to do A. There is no long chain stretching back to things separate from him that give him this constellation of knowledge, desire, and ability; it is due to his *own* knowledge and power and goodness. I see no reason not to say, accordingly, that God is free, even when he does what is best. (434)

My response to Wierenga's proposal is twofold: he is right to thin
there is nothing outside of God that necessitates his doing what h
to be the best action for him to do; he is wrong to think that God is
therefore responsible, and praiseworthy, for his necessarily doing what
he sees to be best. Following Wierenga, let us agree that God's nature as
a necessarily existing, essentially omniscient, omnipotent, perfectly good
being *necessitates* his doing what he sees to be best. Let us also agree that
nothing outside of God brought it about that God has the nature he has,
a nature that necessitates his doing whatever is best. Can we then jump
to the conclusion, as Wierenga does, that God is *free* and *praiseworthy* for
doing what is best? No. If someone's having a certain property or nature
necessitates his behaving in a certain way, it doesn't immediately follow
that he is free when he behaves in that way. Nor does it follow that he is a
fit subject for praise or blame for behaving in that way. And the reason
these things don't follow is that we need first to establish that our agent
is *responsible* for his having the property or nature that necessitates his
behaving in that way. Of course, if his having the property in question is
owing to the independent activity of some agent other than himself, or
the result of factors outside of him over which he has no control, then he
isn't responsible for the behavior that is necessitated by his possession of
the property in question. And, in God's case, we can exclude both of these
seeming possibilities. For no other agent causes God to have the nature he
has. And no factors 'outside of him' over which he has no control bring it
about that he has the nature that he does. But the question still to be
answered is this: Does God cause himself to have the properties constituting his nature, properties that necessitate his always doing what is best?
And if the answer is that God himself is *not responsible* for his possession of
the properties that constitute his nature, then we have thus far not
received a sufficient reason for thinking that God is responsible for, and
to be praised for, the actions he performs and cannot avoid performing,
owing to his possession of the properties constituting his perfect nature.

It is instructive to note, as Jonathan Edwards reminds us, that a moral
saint may be unable to will to accept a bribe; whereas a moral sinner
may be unable to refrain from willing to accept a bribe. I believe,
nevertheless, that it may make sense both to praise the moral saint for
declining the bribe and to blame the moral sinner for accepting the
bribe. For their present 'inabilities' are owing to their earlier constantly
shaping themselves to the point where they are now unable to do
otherwise. But God, of course, never was able to do otherwise. He

never was an infant deity who by strenuous moral efforts so conditioned himself that he later became unable to refrain from doing what he sees to be best. A being who freely over time shapes himself so that he is unable to do less than the best that he can is to be justly praised for his present 'inability' to do less than what he sees to be best. But God always possessed his necessary perfections, and did not acquire them by freely choosing to be the perfect being he is. So, it appears that Wierenga's efforts to provide sufficient ground for thanking and praising God for doing what he cannot avoid doing are simply inadequate to the task.

IX

There is no better way to bring this chapter to a close than by considering an important essay in which Thomas Talbott endeavors to defend God's *freedom* even when there is a best choice for God to make and a best action for him to perform.[48] Of course, as he recognizes, the view he defends is not compatible with a central claim in the *libertarian conception of freedom*.

a Christian view of moral perfection requires that we distinguish between a correct and an incorrect claim that libertarians have made. The correct claim is this: No action that can be traced back to a sufficient cause external to the agent is truly free. The incorrect claim is this: An action is free only if it is logically and psychologically possible for the person who performs it to refrain from it. The latter claim seems to me inconsistent not only with Christian theology, but with widespread intuitions about the nature of moral character as well.[49]

Clearly, both libertarians and Talbott insist that no action that can be traced back to a sufficient cause external to the agent is genuinely free— at least when this claim is rightly understood. For causes that are external to the agent and themselves the product of still earlier causes external to the agent, etc., etc., may stretch back to a time before that agent even existed. And any action that is the causally determined product of causes prior to the existence of the agent can hardly be an action that is genuinely free or an action for which the agent is morally responsible. I take it that it is this thought Talbott has in mind when he writes: 'No action that can be traced back to a sufficient cause external to the agent is truly free.' But it is worth noting that the statement just quoted does not

---

[48] Thomas B. Talbott, 'On the Divine Nature and the Nature of Divine Freedom', *Faith and Philosophy*, 5 (Jan. 1988), 3–24.

[49] Ibid. 17.

itself imply that no action or inaction that has a sufficient cause external to the agent can be one for which the agent is morally responsible. For, to note a classic example, knowing that on hearing the sirens' song he will be tempted beyond his capacity to resist, Odysseus orders his men to tie him to the mast so that at the time he hears their voices he will be unable to yield to the temptation to follow the sirens' call.[50] And yet he is in fact to be morally praised for his being unable to give way to the temptation. He is to be morally praised not because at the time he hears the sirens he was *able* to give way to their call, but refused. He is to be morally praised for *earlier* (and freely) having so arranged things that at the time of hearing the sirens he was then *unable* to give way to them. Here Odysseus is to be morally praised for presently possessing an inability to act because he earlier freely and rightly acted to bring about his own present inability to respond to the sirens' song. And it does not matter that the immediate sufficient cause of his present inability is *external* to himself, lying as it does in the action of those who tied him to the mast. Odysseus is to be morally praised for his present inability even though the immediate cause of that inability is external to Odysseus. He is to be praised because at an earlier time he freely so arranged things that at the time in question his men (the external cause) would render him powerless to respond to the sirens' call.

What we've just noted is that an action (inaction) need not be free in order for the agent to be morally praiseworthy for that action (inaction). Odysseus is, we may say, *derivatively responsible* for his present inaction. For he earlier *freely acted* to bring about his present inaction. But this point does not preclude the truth of the libertarian claim that Talbott agrees with: 'No action that can be traced back to a sufficient cause external to the agent is truly free.' For although Odysseus may be (derivatively) morally responsible for his failure to give way to the sirens' song, at the time when he heard the song he certainly was not free to give way to it, for by then he had been securely tied to the mast.

What then of the libertarian claim that Talbott holds to be false:

> 'An action is free only if it is logically and psychologically possible for the person who performs it to refrain from it'?

Examples in support of this libertarian claim are not difficult to come by. If a young child is exposed to electric shock every time he fails to say 'Yes sir!' when his teacher orders him to do something, it eventually will be

---

[50] *Odyssey* (12. 39, 184).

psychologically impossible for the child to refrain from saying 'Yes sir!' on hearing an order from his teacher. No one who has a command of the language, and knowing the circumstances just described, is likely to insist that when the child, subsequent to this coercive conditioning, says 'Yes sir!' in response to his teacher's command, the child, nevertheless, 'freely' utters that response. For it is not psychologically possible for the child to refrain from so responding. Similarly, since it is *logically impossible* for a person to cause himself to never have existed, consider the 'action' of *causing oneself to never have existed*. Of course, it is only in some Pickwickian sense that we can think of *causing oneself to never have existed* as itself an action, for normally we do not think of logically impossible acts as 'actions'. But insofar as we do count *causing oneself to never have existed* as an 'action', it is clearly impossible for any existing person to perform the action of *causing oneself to never have existed*. Let us now, again in some Pickwickian sense, consider the 'action' *refraining from causing oneself to never have existed*. This is an 'action' that all of us existing persons are constantly performing. And a moment's reflection shows that it is an 'action' that is *logically impossible* for any existing person to not perform. For to fail to perform this action just is to perform an impossible action: *causing oneself to never have existed*. And since no one, not even God, can cause oneself to never have existed, no one, not even God, can *avoid* performing the 'action': *refraining from causing oneself to never have existed*. Indeed, one might well think that since God is a *necessarily* existing being, existing in every possible world, it is particularly obvious that it is impossible for God to perform the action of causing himself to never have existed, and particularly obvious that God *necessarily*, therefore, performs the 'action': *refraining from causing oneself to never have existed*.

In light of these observations, how on earth can Talbott maintain that the child *freely* says 'Yes Sir!' in those circumstances, and God *freely* refrains from causing himself to never have existed? To the first case I believe Talbott's response would be to ask us to consider the question:

> Is it within the child's power to *want* (or *will*) to refrain from saying 'Yes Sir!' on hearing an order from his teacher?

He would then observe that, given the child's painful conditioning, the answer to this question is 'No'. And, so far, this case appears to be similar to the case Talbott gives of the man who is unable to want to torture his wife. Just as it is 'psychologically impossible' for the child to want or will to refrain from saying 'Yes Sir!' on hearing an order from his teacher, so it is 'psychologically impossible' for the man to want or will to torture his wife. There is, however, an important difference between the two cases. In the child's case, the child's present inability to refrain from saying 'Yes Sir!' on hearing an order from his teacher was the result of conditioning *imposed* on the child from an external source; whereas in the man's case the impossibility of his presently wanting to torture his wife is the result of his own earlier *free decision* to spend his life with her, a decision that resulted in his coming to love her in a way that makes it psychologically impossible for him to want to torture her.

The conclusion that one seems justified in reaching is that, unlike the child who cannot refrain from saying 'Yes Sir!' on hearing an order from his teacher, the man may be 'morally praiseworthy' for his present *inability* to torture his wife. He is, as we've earlier suggested, 'derivatively responsible' for this inability because he, earlier in his life, *freely chose* to develop a lasting relationship with the woman who is his wife. But here we should note a possible, significant difference between our man who freely chooses to develop a (hopefully) lasting relationship with the woman who is his wife and Odysseus who freely chose to have his men tie him to the mast so that he is incapable of responding to the sirens' song. Clearly, Odysseus is to be morally praised for subsequently being unable to act, for he earlier freely and rightly acted so as to bring about his own present inability to respond to the sirens' song. But it is very doubtful that our man freely chose to marry the woman who is his wife in order to bring it about that some years later he would love her in a way that makes it psychologically impossible for him to want to torture her. There are long range causal consequences of our free acts that are not themselves freely chosen or consciously foreseen. In Odysseus' case, however, it's clear that the order to his men is freely given so as to achieve the specific end of rendering him unable to respond to the sirens' song. Furthermore, Talbott makes the mistake of confusing a 'free act' with an act for which an agent is, at best, derivatively 'morally responsible'. It is simply a mistake to think that when he hears the sirens' song Odysseus 'freely refrains' from responding. After all, he is unable to respond, freely or unfreely, for he is securely tied to the mast. He is at best *derivatively responsible* for his not responding, for he earlier freely chose to order his men to tie him to the mast so that he would be unable to respond. Similarly, Talbott is simply mistaken in implying that the man *freely refrains* from torturing his beloved wife of twenty years.

At best, we can say that he may be derivatively 'morally responsible' for refraining from torturing her—but, as I've suggested, even this is doubtful since he never acted with the intention of bringing it about that he later will be psychologically unable to torture her.

Talbott, nevertheless, insists that the man *freely refrains* from torturing his beloved wife of twenty years. He does so based on a legitimate distinction between two questions:

> Q1. Does the man in question have the power to strangle his wife should he want or choose to do so?
>
> Q2. Does the man in question have it in his power to want (choose) to strangle his wife?

The answer to Q2, as Talbott agrees, is 'No'. But what of Q1? Here it can be argued that the answer is 'Yes'. And this is a difference between the married man's case and the case of Odysseus when he is tied to the mast. Unlike our man who can't choose to strangle his wife, Odysseus can choose to follow the sirens' call. But even if he chooses, he cannot (being tied to the mast) respond by turning the ship to follow their call. In this respect, then, the Odysseus example is less like the married man example than is the example of the young boy who has been conditioned to say 'Yes sir!' in response to his teacher's command. Just as the married man can't now effectively *will* to strangle his wife, the young boy, given his psychological conditioning, can't now effectively *will* to remain silent upon hearing his teacher's command. The young boy has sufficient control over his organs of speech to not use them should he not will to use them. What he is unable to do, on hearing his teacher's command, is to refrain from willing (choosing) to say 'Yes sir!' Of course, although both are presently incapable of certain choices (choosing to strangle his wife, choosing to refrain from responding 'Yes sir' to his teacher's command) there is this important difference between them. The man's present inability to choose to strangle his wife is partially the result of a much earlier free choice (the choice to marry her), whereas the child's present inability to choose not to say 'Yes sir!' when his teacher orders him to do something may well not be the result of any earlier free choice on his part. But the issue before us is this: does either person (the man, the child) presently perform a *free action* when he (refrains from torturing his wife; responds to his teacher's command with 'Yes sir!')? My point is that it is a mistake to think that in either case the agent performs a free act. Given that he is psychologically incapable of torturing his wife, the man does not *freely* refrain from torturing his wife; and given the severe psychological conditioning, the young child does not *freely* respond 'Yes sir!' to his teacher's command. But, at least in the case of the man, he may be morally praiseworthy for his present inability to strangle his wife. For that present inability is the causal (if unintended) result of his much earlier free act of choosing to spend his life with her. One may be derivatively morally responsible for the causal results of earlier free decisions.

Of course, all of the above is insufficient for Talbott's purposes. To allow that someone is *derivatively morally responsible* for some act he performs or some state he is in does not in the least imply that he performs that act *freely* or *freely* brings it about that he is in that state. What Talbott needs here is a serious argument for why we should think that the man now *freely* refrains from torturing his wife. He also needs a serious argument for why we should think that God now *freely* refrains from performing an act that it would be morally wrong and inconsistent with his perfect nature for him to perform. In neither case is it sufficient to note that each has the raw power to perform such an act *should he will to do it*. For in neither case can the person in question (the man, God) will (choose) to perform that act. In the man's case it is psychologically impossible for him to choose to torture his wife, and in God's case it is logically impossible for him to choose to perform an act that would be morally wrong and inconsistent with his essentially perfect nature for him to perform.

Of course, Talbott is well aware of the objection just made. He himself makes it and replies to it. With respect to God he writes:

> He has the power to perform malicious and cruel acts and therefore has the power to do something such that, were he to do it, he would not be loving and kind at all but malicious and cruel instead. He has this power even though it is logically impossible that he would want to exercise it.[51]

In order to accommodate Talbott we have to make a very sharp distinction between having a power to do X and it being *possible* to exercise that power. All along we have been supposing that it makes no sense to ascribe to God a power to do X if it is logically impossible for God to actually do X. Since it is logically impossible for God to break his solemn promise, it would appear to make no sense to ascribe to God the power to break his solemn promise. Here we may note a view somewhat similar to Talbott's in Samuel Clarke's discussion of God's freedom.

---

[51] 'On the Divine Nature and the Nature of Divine Freedom', 22.

hapter on Clarke we noted his example of God's promising that
ven day he will not destroy the world. The promise *morally*
tes God's refraining from destroying the world on that particular
day. But, says Clarke, it would be absurd to think that God therefore
lacked the physical power on that day to destroy the world.[52] Clarke
claims that God's refraining from destroying the world on that day is
both morally necessary and free. For he both retains the physical power
to destroy the world on that day and also cannot (morally speaking)
break his promise. In favor of Clarke's view we may note that despite his
solemn promise to not destroy the world on that day, God's 'physical
power,' as Clarke calls it, is not somehow sharply diminished when that
day comes around, and miraculously restored come sunrise the next day.
Nevertheless, Clarke readily agrees that it is (morally) impossible for
God to exercise that 'physical power' on that day, for to do so would
deprive him of a property he logically cannot be deprived of: his absolute
moral perfection. So, it looks as though we can choose between two
different ways of describing something that is logically impossible: God's
destroying the world on a day that he previously promised not to destroy
it. One way is to say it is in his power to destroy the world on that day, a
power he *logically* cannot will to exercise. Another way is to say that it
isn't in his power to destroy the world on that day. Either way it turns
out to be strictly impossible for God to destroy the world on that day.

We saw, in Clarke's case, that his effort to preserve God's freedom to
destroy the world on the day he has promised not to destroy it fails. It
fails because Clarke holds to a libertarian conception of freedom, a
conception according to which one is free to do X only if it is in one's
power to refrain from doing X—power to do implies power not to do.
But if we accept, as it seems we must in God's case, that it is logically
impossible for God to *choose* to break his solemn promise on that day,
then it follows that it is not in God's power to choose to break his solemn
promise on that day. It's not in God's power so to choose because such a
choice would amount to divesting himself of his absolute perfection.
And clearly it is not logically possible for God to cease to be absolutely
perfect. Consider now the question: Does God ever freely choose *not* to

[52] 'God's performing his promise is always consequent upon his making it: Yet there is no
connection between them, as between cause and effect: For, not the promise of God, but his
active power, is the alone physical or efficient cause of the performance.' See *Dr. Clarke's
Remarks upon a Book entitled A Philosophical Enquiry Concerning Human Liberty*, in Clarke,
Works (Garland edn.), iv. 9.

do evil? Clarke's own views commit him to a negative answer to this question. For God chooses freely *not* to do something only if it is in his power to choose to do that thing—choosing freely, Clarke insists, logically requires the power to choose otherwise. But it cannot be in anyone's power to make a certain choice if it is logically impossible for that person to make that choice.[53] Therefore, since it is logically impossible for God to choose to do evil, it is not in God's power to choose to do evil. And since it is not in God's power to choose to do evil, it cannot be, for Clarke, that God's choice not to do evil is a free choice. If God chooses not to do evil, he so chooses of necessity, not freely.

How does Talbott escape the argument that appears to be successful in defeating Clarke's attempt to preserve God's freedom to destroy the world on a day that he has promised not to destroy it? Talbott escapes the argument against Clarke by refusing to accept the common view that power extends only to what it is logically possible for one to do. According to Talbott it makes perfect sense to say that it is in God's power to choose to do evil, to choose to break his solemn promise not to destroy the world on a given day, etc. According to Talbott it is no more difficult for God to choose to do evil than it is for him to choose to do good, no more difficult for God to choose to break his solemn promise than it is for him to choose to keep his solemn promise—never mind that it is logically impossible for God to choose do evil, and never mind that it is logically impossible for God to choose to break his solemn promise. Only by such extraordinary distortion of the common use of 'power to do' and 'power to choose' is Talbott able to preserve God's 'perfect freedom' to choose to do less than the best, when there is a best that he can do. But surely this is an instance of 'language gone on holiday'.

There remains, however, the valid point Talbott makes in pointing out that the married man who is now so deeply in love with his wife that he is simply incapable of strangling her, or even choosing to do so, is nevertheless in some way morally responsible for his present inability to strangle her, and indeed may be subject to moral praise for his present inability. But in this case it is important to note that the man's present inability is the result of an earlier *free choice* on his part, the choice to commit himself to her in marriage. Of course, not every such free choice

---

[53] *If there is no possible world in which a person makes a certain choice, it cannot be that the person, nevertheless, has it within his power to make that choice.*

to marry results in such an inability. But the free choice here may reasonably be thought to have played an important causal role in the development of his present inability to strangle her. So, although he is not now able to choose to strangle her, he is, nevertheless, morally praiseworthy for that inability because an earlier *free choice* of his played an important causal role in the development of his present inability to strangle her. Had he at no previous time been free to do anything that would causally contribute to his now being in this state of inability, he would not deserve *moral praise* for his present inability to strangle her.

What then of God's inability to do less than what is best, given that there is a best to be done? Does this divine inability share the crucial feature that grounds moral praise of the husband's inability to choose to strangle his beloved wife of many years? Is it in some way the causal result of a divine free choice? It hardly seems so. God's nature logically precludes his ever doing less than the best, given that there is a best to be done. We can say that it is part of the 'nature' of the loving husband of many years that makes it 'impossible' for him to strangle his wife. But here the resemblance between the two cases ends. For the man, as a result (along with other factors) of an earlier *free choice* to marry and live with the woman who now is his wife, played an important causal role in bringing it about that his psychological nature is now such as to preclude his even choosing to strangle his wife, let alone doing so. But the Christian God Talbott is discussing never caused himself to come to have the nature of being an absolutely perfect being. It's not as though he was once an infant deity able to do good or evil, who then slowly developed himself to where he is now incapable of breaking a solemn promise and of choosing to do evil. He had no role at all in bringing about his having the perfect nature he has. And it is that perfect nature that precludes his ever choosing to do less than the best. Thus, the analogy on which Talbot's argument rests fails at a crucial point. It appears that only if God is in some way causally responsible for his own perfect nature can we be justified in morally praising God for the perfect acts required by his essential nature.

7

Can God Be the Cause of His Own Nature?

On the assumption that God (the supremely perfect being) exists and that there is a best, creatable world, we've reached the conclusion that God is neither free not to create a world nor free to create a world less than the best creatable world. Indeed, God would of necessity create the best of the creatable worlds, leaving us with no basis for thanking him, or praising him for creating the world he does. For given that God exists and that there is a best creatable world, God's nature as an omnipotent, omniscient, perfectly good being would require him to create that best world. Doing less than the best he can do—create the best world— would be inconsistent with his being the perfect being he is. But what if, strange as it may seem, God is *causally responsible* for having the perfect nature that he has? What if God *creates* his nature, and, by virtue of having created it, is thereby causally responsible for his own nature? Such a view, if it were correct, might provide a way out of our problem. For we have been assuming all along that no being is, or can be, responsible for having the nature it has. And, given that this assumption is correct, what logically follows from God's possessing the nature (being supremely perfect) he does—i.e, his creating the best possible world— can no more be up to God, something he is responsible for, than is his nature as a supremely perfect being something that is up to him, something he is responsible for. But against our assumption, Thomas Morris has argued[1] that God does create his nature and, therefore, is causally responsible for his nature. Suppose, for the moment that Morris

---

[1] Thomas V. Morris, *Anselmian Explorations* (Notre Dame, Ind.: University of Notre Dame Press, 1987), ch. 9.

is right: that God is responsible for his own nature. Well, then, since God is responsible for his nature, he may then be responsible for what is required by his nature. In short, God may be responsible for his creation of the best world. So, it seems to matter whether God is responsible for having the nature he has.

Of course, in the broad sense of the expression 'a person's nature' someone may be responsible for his nature, or at least part of it. A person with a naturally friendly disposition toward strangers may have played a role in developing his 'nature' to be friendly toward strangers, and thus may bear some responsibility for his 'nature' to be friendly toward others. But no one, it seems, is responsible for being the basic sort of entity one is—a human being, for example. Thus, even God, so it is generally thought, is not causally responsible for his basic nature—his being omnipotent, omniscient, and perfectly good. Of course, unlike humans, God, if he exists, does not inherit his nature from prior beings. For God is eternal and not generated by other gods. From eternity this uncreated being has been omnipotent, omniscient, and perfectly good. These properties constitute his intrinsic nature.[2] Thus it seems that no one, including God, could be causally responsible for God's having the basic properties that are constitutive of his nature. Against this view, however, Thomas Morris argues that there is nothing logically or metaphysically objectionable about God's creating, and thereby being causally responsible for, his own basic nature. He does, however, wish to avoid having to claim that God is the cause of himself. As he says, 'the very idea of self-causation or self-creation is almost universally characterized as absurd, incoherent, or worse.'[3] What Morris means here is that although it is absurd to think that God causes *himself* to exist from all eternity, it is not absurd, in his judgment, to suppose that God (1) causes there to be such properties as omnipotence, omniscience, and perfect goodness, and (2) causes himself to eternally possess these properties.

It may be helpful toward understanding Morris's view of divine causation to consider an example of causation in which a cause need not be temporally prior to its effect. For if we come to accept the idea that a cause need not be temporally prior to its effect, we will have removed one source of resistance to Morris's claim that God can be the

---

[2] Actually, these properties constitute only part of his nature. Being eternal, omnipresent, unchanging, are also among the properties essential to the God of traditional theism.

[3] Morris, *Anselmian Explorations*, 174.

cause of his nature even though there is no time at which God exists but his nature does not. Among the medieval philosophers there was a lively debate concerning whether the world is eternal or had a beginning. Aquinas was among those philosophers who thought that the philosophical arguments for the world's having a beginning were not fully convincing. Of course, as a Christian philosopher he believed that the world in fact had a beginning because he believed that God has revealed that truth to us. So, for him it was a truth of faith that the world had a beginning. His point was only that the world's having a beginning is not a truth of reason. For reason alone, in his judgment, is unable to prove that the world had a beginning. Nevertheless, Aquinas was convinced that reason alone could prove that the world was caused to exist by God—and he was convinced that this is so, and would be so, even if it should be the case that the world in fact never had a beginning. So, Aquinas, along with a number of other philosophers, thought that it is possible for an eternal cause to have an eternal effect. Moreover, these medieval thinkers gave hypothetical examples of the sort of causation they had in mind. Here is an example of the sort favored by medievals. Suppose that while walking at the seashore we come upon a very large stone resting on the sand. Moving the stone slightly, we observe an indentation in the sand where the stone has been resting. If one were to ask what caused that indentation in the sand, the reasonable answer would be the large, heavy stone lying there at that very place. Accepting this answer, what would we say if we then imagined both that the seashore with its sandy beach had been there from eternity and that the heavy, large stone also had been there from eternity in that very same spot? I suspect we might say that the stone has been *eternally* causing that indentation in the sand. And we might say this even though there never was a time at which the stone and the indentation were not present at that particular spot on the sandy beach. By such examples as this, some of the medieval philosophers came to believe that an eternal object could be the cause of an effect that is itself eternal in the sense of never having begun to exist.

As useful as the stone indentation-in-the-sand example may be in helping us to understand Morris's claim about God being the cause of his own nature, there are some important differences between the two examples. In the stone indentation-in-the-sand example, one thing (the stone) is said to be eternally causing an effect (the indentation) in something else (the sand). Moreover, it would be possible for the stone to exist even if the sandy beach did not. In Morris's proposal, God is said to be the cause of something (his nature) that God cannot possibly exist without. And, to us, it may seem impossible for any being to be the cause of something (its nature) which that very being cannot exist without. Therefore, it may seem impossible for God to be causally responsible for his nature. Indeed (to stress the point again), since God's nature consists of his essential properties, properties he must have in order to exist, it seems absurd to even suggest that God is causally responsible for these properties and for his possession of them. Morris responds to this objection by noting that God necessarily exists and therefore always has his essential properties. So, we should not think that God could exist without his nature and then cause the properties constituting his nature (absolute goodness, absolute power, and absolute knowledge) and cause himself to possess them. Nevertheless, Morris claims that the fact that God can exist only if his nature also exists doesn't preclude God's being causally responsible for his nature. He simply is always causally responsible for these properties and his essential possession of them. As Morris puts it: 'It just seems to be that there is nothing logically or metaphysically objectionable about God's creating his own nature. . . .'[4] However, he then raises the following objection to his view: 'But what of the apparent implication that if God creates his nature, and the existence of his nature is logically sufficient for his existence, then he creates himself?'[5] Morris takes this objection seriously, allowing I believe, that it is (so far as he knows) logically inconceivable even for God to create, or be causally responsible for, himself. (And as we've noted above, many philosophers hold that it is simply incoherent to suppose that something could cause itself to exist.) Suppose, then, we agree with Morris that nothing, including God, can cause its own existence. How then does Morris seek to rebut the objection that if God is causally responsible for his essential properties he is thereby causally responsible for his own existence, for creating himself? Here is his response.

God stands in a relation of logical dependence to his nature (a trivial result of the strict necessity of both relata). His nature stands in a relation of causal dependence to him. It simply does not follow that God stands in a relation of causal dependence to himself. Relations of logical dependence are always transitive. Relations of continuous causal dependence are always transitive. But we have no good reason to think that transitivity always holds across these two relations. If

---

[4] Morris, *Anselmian Explorations,* 176.   [5] Ibid.

God creates some bachelor, the existence of this bachelor is logically sufficient for the existence of some unmarried man. It follows that God creates some unmarried man. But the transitivity we thus see across the causal and logical dependence relations holds only in case the unmarried man is one and the same individual as the bachelor. Unless the doctrine of divine simplicity is true, God is not identical with his nature. Since I have rejected the doctrine of divine simplicity, I can reject as well the inference that from God's nature causally depending on God, and God's logically depending on his nature, it follows that God causally depends on himself. Thus the view that God is absolute creator of everything distinct from himself does not entail that God is self-caused, or self-created.[6]

The objection Morris considers can be put as follows.

A bachelor is created by God.
An unmarried man's existence is logically dependent on the existence of a bachelor.
Therefore,
An unmarried man is created by God.

Morris points out that for the transitivity to hold here it must be that the unmarried man referred to in the conclusion is one and the same individual as the bachelor picked out in the first premiss. Similarly, he argues that for the following argument to be valid,

God's nature is causally dependent on God.
God is logically dependent on God's nature.
Therefore,
God is causally dependent on God.

it must be that God's nature just is God. But Morris rejects this inference since he rejects the doctrine of divine simplicity: that God is identical to his nature. 'Since I have rejected the doctrine of divine simplicity, I can reject as well the inference that from God's nature depending on God, and God's logically depending on his nature, it follows that God causally depends on himself.'[7]

I think there is a simpler way of restructuring the above argument so that it yields the conclusion [God is causally dependent on God] than to appeal to the doctrine of divine simplicity: that God is identical to his nature. If we simply replace 'logically' in the second premiss with the weaker 'causally', the resulting argument will possess the virtue of

---

[6] Morris, *Anselmian Explorations*, 176.   [7] Ibid

validity providing 'being causally dependent' is a transitive relation.[8] But Morris would reject the claim that God is causally dependent on his nature. Alternatively, one might argue that 'X is logically dependent on Y' implies 'X is causally dependent on Y'. But although 'logically implies' is a stronger relation than 'causally implies', it does not entail it. And so I conclude from this brief inquiry that Morris appears to be successful in arguing that from the premiss that God's nature stands in a relation of causal dependence to him it does not follow that God need stand in a relation of causal dependence to himself.

Before we agree with Morris that God can be causally responsible for his nature (his necessarily being perfectly good, all-powerful, and all-knowing) we should note a further disparity between the stone indentation-in-the-sand example and God's being the cause of his own nature. As we've already observed, one thing (the stone) is said to be eternally causing an effect (the indentation) in something else (the sand); whereas in the case of God's causing his own nature, God is said to be eternally causing an effect not in something else but in himself—i.e., his eternal and necessary possession of the properties constituting his nature. Suppose we now ask the question: In virtue of *what* is the stone eternally causing that indentation in the sand? Here there appears to be an answer in terms of a property possessed by the stone—the property of always having been located at just that spot in the sand. And it is by virtue of the stone's having that property that we can explain the stone's possession of the property of eternally causing that indentation in the sand.[9] But when we ask the question: In virtue of *what* is God eternally causing his possession of the properties constituting his nature?, there seems to be no further divine property available to provide the explanation. And thereby is revealed a further difference between our stone/indentation in the sand example and the example of God/his nature. Moreover, this difference may raise a difficulty for Morris's view that God is the cause of *all* the divine properties. For it now appears that God is not the cause of his having the property of *causing his possession of the properties constituting his nature*. Even here, however, one might suggest that it is God's necessarily willing his being perfect that explains God's causing his

---

[8] A relation R is transitive just in case if A has R to B, and B has R to C, it logically follows that A has R to C.

[9] And here, if we wished to explain why the stone has the property of always having been located at just that spot in the sand we would presumably have to appeal to something other than the stone.

possession of the properties constituting his nature. But suppose we then ask: in virtue of what does God have the property of necessarily willing his being perfect? Here we approach a dilemma: If we say in virtue of nothing: i.e., God just necessarily has the property of necessarily willing his being perfect, then it isn't true that God is both the cause of his divine properties and the cause of his possession of those properties. For one of the divine properties—the property of necessarily willing his being perfect—is a property God has but doesn't cause himself to have. So, the dilemma confronting Morris seems to be this: either God has a property he does not cause himself to have or there is an infinite regress of properties that God must cause himself to have.[10] Perhaps Morris will accept the second horn of this dilemma and view the regress as harmless to his view. Thus we would have the following infinite series:

> God causes his possession of property P (necessarily willing his being perfect)
> God causes his possession of property P1 (causing his possession of property P)
> God causes his possession of property P2 (causing his possession of property P1)
> God causes his possession of property P3 (causing his possession of property P2)
> etc., etc., . . .

It is no simple matter to determine whether an infinite regress of the sort just described is benign or vicious. But let's suppose we can allow Morris everything he argues for on this issue—that God is creatively responsible for the existence of properties, relations, mathematical truths, logical truths, necessary states of affairs, possible states of affairs, etc.—and still insist that God's causing of his nature was not itself *up to God.* For, on Morris's view, although God creates the entire framework of reality, it was not up to God whether to create the framework he did or some other framework instead, or even not to create any part of the framework he created. God never had a choice about creating this framework or any part of it for, in Morris's words, 'God's creation of the framework of reality is both eternal and necessary—it never was, never will be, and could not have been, other than it

---

[10] I'm here considering only those properties that are intrinsic to God. If God exists he, of course, has properties that creatures may cause him to have—for example, being discussed in philosophy of religion courses, being thought about by theologians, etc.

is.'[11] Clearly, if God's creation of the framework of reality never could have been other than it is, then God never had any choice about creating the framework of reality. He created it of *necessity*, and *not freely*.

Morris is very much aware of the difficulty just noted. His response to it is direct and to the point. Referring to God's creation of the framework of reality, he writes:

> But there is a sense, a different sense, in which even it can be considered *free*. It is an activity which is conscious, intentional, and neither constrained nor compelled by anything existing independent of God and his causally efficacious power. The necessity of his creating the framework is not imposed on him from without, but rather is a feature and result of the nature of his own activity itself, which is a function of what he is.[12]

Morris recognizes, I believe, that the primary sense in which an agent is *free* in performing an action requires that the agent either (*a*) could have refrained from performing that action or, at least, (*b*) could have refrained from causing his decision to perform that action. And it is this sense of being free in performing an action that constitutes a necessary condition for an agent's being morally responsible for an action he performs. (Morris, I believe, shares the view I express here: that the libertarian idea of freedom is essential to moral responsibility.) The importance of including condition (*b*), in addition to (*a*), is to allow an action to be one for which the agent is morally responsible in special situations in which the agent performs that action but could not have refrained from performing it.[13] For there may be occasions when an agent performs an action but for reasons unknown to the agent could not have avoided performing the action. Suppose, for example, that a mad scientist has gained access to your brain and, unknown to you, is prepared to cause certain changes in your brain that directly cause you to perform action A just in case you are about to not perform action A on your own. If the mad scientist sees events occurring in your brain that indicate that you will not perform action A on your own, the mad scientist will intervene and directly cause you to do A. But suppose that what the mad scientist sees is that you will cause your doing action A. Here the mad scientist is ready to interfere and cause you to do A—should you be about to refrain from doing A. But, as it turns out,

---

[11] Ibid. 170.   [12] Ibid. 170–1.

[13] See Harry Frankfurt's classic essay 'Alternate Possibilities and Moral Responsibility,' *Journal of Philosophy*, 16 (1969), 828–39.

the mad scientist doesn't have to interfere, for he sees that you will cause your doing action A on your own. Our intuitions tell us that you are morally responsible for doing A in these circumstances. For the truth is that no action on the part of the mad scientist is necessary. If he hadn't been there at all, you would have decided and acted as you did for reasons of your own. And yet, given the mad scientist and his control of events in your brain, you could not have refrained from doing A. But this case is dealt with by condition (*b*). For in the case at hand *you* could have refrained from *causing* your decision and action of killing Jones. Of course, had you been about to not cause that decision and action, the mad scientist's machine would have intervened and caused you to decide to kill Jones, resulting in your action of killing Jones. But then it is the mad scientist, and not you, who is responsible for your decision to kill Jones and your action of killing Jones. In this case, you couldn't refrain from killing Jones, but you could refrain from causing your decision to kill Jones and the action following on that decision.

In the primary sense of 'being free in performing an action'—the sense required for moral responsibility—the power *not to have caused* the *decision to act* is necessary. For without such power the agent has no control over his performing an action. And without such power on God's part with respect to his 'creation' of the framework of reality, it makes no sense, I submit, to thank God or praise God for creating that eternal framework. Only in some Pickwickian sense can we view God as 'morally responsible' for the creation of the framework of reality. This is not to deny the important distinction Morris draws between God and the necessary truths constituting the framework of reality. God is causally active in a way in which a necessary truth such as Clarke's example—there being innocent beings who do not suffer eternally is necessarily better than there being innocent beings who do suffer eternally—is not. But for all Morris says about the matter, God has no choice but to form the thought that there being innocent beings who do not suffer eternally is necessarily better than there being innocent beings who do suffer eternally. And God has no choice but to acknowledge the truth of this thought. Neither of these doings on God's part—having that thought, acknowledging its truth—is any more up to God than it is up to a leaf whether or not it moves when the wind blows against it. Neither the leaf nor God has any choice in the matter.

As we've seen, Morris believes that God can be the cause of his own nature. By this he means that God is both the cause of the properties (omniscience, omnipotence, and perfect goodness) and the cause of God's having those properties. Indeed, Morris holds that God is the cause of all the elements constituting the framework of reality. Moreover, I believe Morris is well aware that God has no control over his causing the framework of reality or causing the divine properties and his having those properties. The primary sense in which we say that an agent is free in doing something requires that at the time he did it the agent could have avoided doing what he did or could have avoided causing his decision to do that thing. It is this sense of having control that many philosophers hold to be essential if an agent is to be morally responsible for his decision and action.[14] And it is because God is not free (in the sense required for moral responsibility) when he performs actions necessitated by his absolute perfections that it makes no sense to thank God or praise him for doing those actions. It is true, however, as Morris points out, that God's having no choice either about creating the framework of reality or about having the properties of absolute power, knowledge, and goodness, does not result from something else imposing this framework and properties upon him. And this seems to distinguish God from the leaf that has no choice about moving when the wind blows. The necessity of the leaf's moving is imposed on it by something else (the wind). The necessity of God's doing what is best is imposed by God's nature, his being perfectly good, something that is internal to God and something that, on Morris's account, God himself causes, but had no choice about causing. So, unlike the leaf's being caused to move by something else (the wind), God, we may say, necessarily does what is best because given his perfect nature he cannot do other than the best. And although God causes his eternal possession of his perfect nature he had no choice about eternally causing himself to be perfect. Let's then ask ourselves this question: Does God have any more of a choice about doing what is best than the leaf, were it endowed with consciousness, would have about moving when the wind blows? I'm afraid the answer must be 'No'. For each necessarily does what it does as a result of factors over which neither has any control. And that being so, God is no more

---

[14] I ignore here cases of 'derivative responsibility', where an agent freely and knowingly causes himself to be in a situation where he is caused to will to do X and cannot refrain from willing to do X. In such cases the agent can be said, in a derivative sense, to be morally responsible for what he now must do, for the agent freely put himself in circumstances that he knew would necessitate his act.

morally responsible for choosing to do what is best than our leaf is for moving when the wind blows.

Against the prevailing theme of this book—*that the greatest possible being can create a world only if there is no better creatable world*—we've thus far considered a number of objections and given what I hope are sensible replies. But as we've seen, the issue of whether this basic theme is true can be divided into two parts depending on whether there is a best possible, creatable world or whether for any creatable world there is a better creatable world. If we suppose that there is a best creatable world, it is difficult to think of any good reason why the best possible being would choose to create an inferior world when it could have chosen to create the very best world. The only argument that seems at all promising is Adams's argument, an argument based on an inferior world providing God a greater opportunity to manifest his grace. However, as we've seen, Adam's argument establishes, at best, that God need not be doing anything morally wrong in creating some world other than the best world. But this isn't quite the same thing as showing that God's perfect goodness does not render it *necessary* that he create the best world he can. For one being may be morally better than another even though it is not better by virtue of the performance of some *obligation* that the other failed to perform. It may be morally better by virtue of performing some *supererogatory act*—a good act beyond the call of duty—that the other being could have but did not perform. Therefore, a being who creates a better world than another being may be morally better, even though the being who creates the inferior world does not thereby do anything wrong.

When we turn to the no best world part of our question it is more difficult to argue for an affirmative answer to our question. For it is clear that in order to create a world a creator must select a world that is inferior to another world he could have created instead. The hope of doing the best that he can is a false hope. On the supposition that for any creatable world there is a better creatable world, I've argued that God cannot exist and be the creator of a world. For no matter what world he creates he will do less good than he can. And it is simply impossible for God to intentionally choose to do less good than he is able to do. This response to God's predicament in the no best world scenario may seem questionable. For many of the great theologians and philosophers in the major religions of the West claim that God is a *necessary being*, that it is impossible for God not to exist. And for those who adopt the view that

God's existence is absolutely necessary it is simply not a possible solution to the problem to suggest that God cannot exist if there is no best world for him to create. For if God's existence is absolutely necessary there simply cannot be any possible situation such that its being actual would preclude the existence of God. In short, those who hold that God necessarily exists are more likely to brush aside the objections we've raised in the no best world scenario than to concede that God cannot do less good than he is able to do. Thus we seem to have reached a stalemate: I maintain that it is impossible for God to exist and create an inferior world when he could have created a better world; my opponent maintains that in the no best world scenario God would be free to create some good world even though there is an unlimited number of better worlds any one of which he could have created instead. Must matters be left here with a conflict of intuitions? Or is there, perhaps, a solution that may be agreeable to both sides of the dispute? I will suggest such a solution that rests on a thesis advanced by Thomas Morris.

When we think of all the possible worlds in terms of their respective degrees of goodness or badness we may be led to conclude that among possible worlds there are worlds that are good, worlds that are bad, and worlds that are neutral—neither good nor bad. A reason sometimes given to think that there are no bad worlds is that badness or evil has been held to be nothing more than the absence of good. But an unhappy person is not just a person who isn't in a state of happiness. For one may be neither happy nor unhappy. And so too for good and bad. Good and bad are opposites, like hot and cold, or happiness and unhappiness. A world composed of nothing more than some stones whirling in space is certainly not a good world in the sense of including instances of qualities that are intrinsically good: happiness, love, beauty, justice, and the like. But neither does the stone world include instances of qualities that are intrinsically bad: unhappiness, hate, ugliness, injustice, and the like. So, it seems clear that while some possible worlds may be good worlds in the sense of containing good states of affairs that outweigh any bad states of affairs those worlds may contain, other worlds may be bad worlds in the sense of containing bad states of affairs that outweigh any good states of affairs those worlds contain. And still other worlds may be neutral by virtue of containing no intrinsically good or intrinsically bad states of affairs, or by containing a balance between good and bad states of affairs. And when we think of God creating a world we mean that God makes actual the states of affairs that constitute that world. And since God is perfectly good and omniscient we would suppose that he would not create (actualize) any of the bad worlds. Moreover, on a theistic view of things the only way in which one of these worlds becomes the actual world is by virtue of God's creating it, making actual, directly or indirectly, the states of affairs constituting it.[15] And that perhaps is all we need to understand in order to grasp the significance of Morris's thesis concerning the role God may play in determining what worlds are really possible, as opposed to just seeming to be possible.

The reason for thinking that possible worlds will include good worlds, bad worlds, and worlds neither good nor bad is that such worlds can be *conceived* by us as internally consistent, involving only states of affairs that are consistent with one another. But on Morris's view, mere conceivability is insufficient for determining that a world is genuinely possible. Here is what he says.

... many impossibilities are consistently describable *to a point*, and in this sense conceivable. Thus for reasons having nothing to do with theism, we must always carefully distinguish between conceivability and genuine possibility. Something is genuinely possible in the broadly logical sense, and, we might say, in the fullest sense conceivable, only if its actuality would be compatible with all the necessary features of reality, including for example the laws of mathematics. Among those necessary features of reality, the Anselmian will hold the nature of God to be the most important of constraints on what is possible.[16]

What Morris is telling us here is that someone who holds that God (a being whose nature is to be absolutely perfect in every way) necessarily exists is within his rights to also hold that if what seems to be a possible world—e.g., our simple world W9 in which total hatred prevails among its creatures—is a world whose creation would be *inconsistent* with the absolute perfections of this being, then that world cannot possibly be actualized by God and is, therefore, not a genuine possibility. And what we are to glean from this point is that all sorts of 'possible worlds'—all the worlds that are bad on the whole—are such that while they may seem to us to be genuinely possible, they really aren't possible in the

---

[15] If a state of affairs consists of some human being's freely helping another human being, God cannot directly bring about that state of affairs by creating that person and 'causing' him to help another being. But by knowing in advance what that person will freely do in that situation, God may be able to indirectly bring about that state of affairs by bringing it about that that person is in that situation.

[16] Morris, *Anselmian Explorations*, 47.

theistic framework. For their creation by God is inconsistent with God's necessarily being the perfect being that he is.

Morris nicely captures the essence of this view of God by noting that such a God 'is a delimiter of possibilities'.

If there is a being who exists necessarily, and is necessarily omnipotent, omniscient, and good, then many states of affairs which otherwise would represent genuine possibilities, and by all non-theistic tests of logic and semantics do represent possibilities, are strictly impossible in the strongest sense. In particular, worlds containing certain sorts or amounts of disvalue or evil are metaphysically ruled out by the nature of God, divinely precluded from the realm of real possibility.[17]

Return now to our earlier contention that possible worlds include good worlds, neutral worlds, and bad worlds. In addition we might think that just as for every good world there is a better possible world, so too for every bad world there is a world whose degree of badness is greater. Morris will allow that such worlds are conceivable. But since he holds that God is a delimiter of possibilities and that it is impossible for God to create a world that is a bad world, the bad worlds we conceive of are not, at least for the theist, genuinely possible. For the only way such worlds could be genuinely possible is for it to be possible for God to create them. But God's perfect nature precludes him from creating such worlds. Therefore, such worlds aren't really possible all things considered.

Morris's general point here strikes me as sound. If p is necessarily true and q is inconsistent with p, then, even though we can conceive of q and q seems to us to be paradigm case of a genuine possibility, q isn't really possible at all. So, if there is a necessarily perfect being who necessarily exists, then even though we can conceive of a bad world, that bad world is really not a *possible world* given that for a world to be actual it must be actualized by the necessarily perfect being. Consider, for example, a world in which nearly all the sentient beings have lives so full of suffering that it would be better had they never existed. Such a world is a bad world. Is this world, so understood, a possible world? It certainly seems to be. But given that a possible world can be actual only if it is created by a necessarily perfect being, and such a being necessarily exists, then that world really isn't a possible world, it only seems to be possible. Of course, what is sauce for the goose is sauce for the gander. If this bad

[17] Ibid. 48.

world which certainly seems to be possible really is a possible world, then it is simply *impossible* that there is a necessarily perfect being who is necessarily the creator of any world that is actual. Which then are we more sure of: that some bad world is genuinely possible or that there necessarily exists a being who is necessarily omnipotent, omniscient, and perfectly good? The former is a 'delimiter of necessities' just as the latter is a 'delimiter of possibilities'. Just as what is necessary precludes certain 'possibilities', so does what is possible preclude certain 'necessities'. The theist begins with God as a necessary being and concludes that a bad world isn't even a possibility. The non-theist begins with the possibility of there being a bad world and concludes that there is no essentially perfect being that necessarily exists.

Suppose we accept Morris's view about God as a delimiter of possibilities. Suppose, that is, that we agree with him that if there is a being who exists necessarily, and is necessarily omnipotent, omniscient, and good, then many states of affairs which otherwise would have been possible are strictly impossible. If so, then if we know that there is such a being we should agree that there are no possible worlds that are overall bad worlds. For such a world is possible only if it is possible for God to actualize that world. But God's necessary perfections preclude him from actualizing a bad world. Therefore, such a world is not really a possible world.

Having adopted Morris's view that God is a delimiter of possibilities, suppose we now return to the stalemate between the view I've argued for:

> It is impossible for God to exist and create an inferior world when he could have created a better world;

and the view my opponent maintains:

> God is free to create some good world even though there is an unlimited number of better worlds any one of which he could have created instead.

My opponent may well agree with me that given God's absolute perfection God could not create a world less than the best world. In short, if there is a best world all things considered, we may both agree with Leibniz and Clarke that God will necessarily create the best world. (Of course, there remains the problem of explaining the precise sense in which God could be *free* in creating the best possible world.) It is only when we come to the no best world scenario that our views clash so profoundly. But perhaps Morris has shown us a way to resolve the problem. God is the *delimiter of possibilities*. Thus, if God exists then just as the series of decreasingly good possible worlds has a limit—a world that is the least good world—so the series of increasingly good possible worlds has a limit—the best possible world. A creator that is necessarily good could not possibly create a less than good world. So, given that this being is a delimiter of possibilities, there are no possible worlds that are not good worlds. Furthermore, a necessarily perfect being could not possibly create a world that is less good than some other world it could create. So, given that this being creates a world and is a delimiter of possibilities, the world he creates cannot be one than which there is a better creatable world. Thus, following the path that Morris has pointed out, we conclude that God's necessary existence and necessary perfections would rule out two seeming possibilities: (1) there being possible worlds that are bad; (2) there being an unending series of increasingly better worlds.[18] In fact, if God exists, his necessary existence and perfection would require either a best possible world or a number of worlds equally good and none better. In the former case, God would of necessity create the best possible world. In the latter case, God could possess a degree of freedom with respect to which of the equally best worlds he selects for creation. But, as we've noted in the previous chapter, even this degree of freedom, as Wierenga points out, 'amounts to saying that God is free only *when it does not matter what he does*'.

---

[18] Keith Yandell has argued that God's necessary existence and necessary perfections also raise problems with respect to the important Christian doctrine that God became incarnate in Jesus Christ. For Christianity holds that Jesus was tempted, which appears to imply that Jesus could sin. Yandell concludes that Jesus did not sin is, therefore, best viewed as a logically contingent truth. But since Jesus *is* God, this hardly seems possible if the being who is God necessarily exists and is necessarily perfect. See Yandell's 'Divine Necessity and Divine Goodness' in Thomas V. Morris (ed.), *Divine and Human Action* (Ithaca, NY and London: Cornell University Press, 1988), 313–44.

Bibliography

Adams, Marilyn McCord and Adams, Robert M. (eds.), *The Problem of Evil* (Oxford: Oxford University Press, 1990).

Adams, Robert M., 'Must God Create the Best?', *Philosophical Review*, 81 (1972), 317–32.

——*Leibniz: Determinist, Theist, Idealist* (Oxford: Oxford University Press, 1994).

Aquinas, Thomas, *Summa Theologica* (1256–72), in *The Basic Writings of Saint Thomas Aquinas*, ed. Anton C. Pegis (New York: Random House, 1945).

—— *Summa contra Gentiles* (1260), tr. Anton C. Pegis (New York: Doubleday & Company, Inc., 1955).

Aristotle, *Nicomachean Ethics*, in *The Basic Works of Aristotle*, ed. Richard Mckeon (New York: Random House, 1941).

Augustine, *The City of God* (413–27), tr. M. Dods (New York: Random House, 1948).

Bard, Jennifer S., 'Unjust Rules for Insanity', *The New York Times*, 27 August 2002.

Blumenthal, D., 'Is the Best Possible World Possible?', *Philosophical Review*, 84 (1975), 163–77.

Chisholm, Roderick M., 'The Defeat of Good and Evil', *Proceeding of the American Philosophical Association*, 42 (1968–9), 21–38. Reprinted in Adams and Adams (eds.), *The Problem of Evil*.

Clarke, Samuel, *A Demonstration of the Being and Attributes of God* (1705; 9th edn., London, printed by W. Botham for John and Paul Knapton, 1738).

——*Works: British Philosophers and Theologians of the 17th and 18th Centuries*, vols. i–iv (1738; New York: Garland Press, 1978).

—— and Leibniz, Gottfried, *The Leibniz–Clarke Correspondence* (1717), ed. H. G. Alexander (Manchester: Manchester University Press, 1956).

Davies, Brian, *The Thought of Thomas Aquinas* (Oxford: Clarendon Press, 1993).

Edwards, Jonathan, *Freedom of the Will* (1754), ed. Paul Ramsey (New Haven: Yale University Press, 1957).

Flint Thomas P., 'The Problem of Divine Freedom', *American Philosophical Quarterly*, 20 (1983), 255–64.

Frankfurt, Harry G., 'Alternate Possibilities and Moral Responsibility', *Journal of Philosophy*, 66 (1969), 829–39.

Grover, Steven, 'Why Only the Best is Good Enough', *Analysis*, 48 (1988), 224.

Hasker, William, 'Must God Do His Best?', *International Journal for Philosophy of Religion*, 16 (1984), 213–23.

——— *God, Time, and Knowledge* (Ithaca, NY: Cornell University Press, 1989).

——— 'The Freedom and Goodness of God', in his *Providence, Evil, and the Openness of God* (Routledge, forthcoming).

Howard-Snyder, Daniel and Frances, 'How an Unsurpassable Being Can Create a Surpassable World', *Faith and Philosophy*, 11 (1994), 260–8.

——— ——— 'The *Real* Problem of No Best World', *Faith and Philosophy*, 13 (1996), 422–5.

Kretzmann, N., 'A General Problem of Creation' in Scott MacDonald (ed.), *Being and Goodness* (Ithaca, NY and London: Cornell University Press, 1990).

——— 'A Particular Problem of Creation', in Scott MacDonald (ed.), *Being and Goodness* (Ithaca, NY and London: Cornell University Press, 1990).

Langtry, Bruce, 'God and the Best', *Faith and Philosophy*, 13 (1996), 311–28.

Leibniz, Gottfried, *New Essays on Human Understanding* (1704), abridged edn., tr. and ed. P. Remnant and J. Bennett (Cambridge: Cambridge University Press, 1982).

——— *Theodicy* (1710; LaSalle, Ill: Open Court, 1985).

——— 'Monadology' in (1714), *Leibniz Selections*, ed. Philip P. Wiener (New York: Charles Scribner's Sons, 1951).

Lovejoy, Arthur O., *The Great Chain of Being* (1963; Cambridge, Mass.: Harvard University Press, 1978).

Menssen, Sandra and Sullivan, Thomas, 'Must God Create?', *Faith and Philosophy*, 3 (1995), 321–41.

Moore, G. E., *Principia Ethica* (Cambridge: Cambridge University Press, 1903).

Morris, Thomas V., *Anselmian Explorations* (Notre Dame, Ind.: University of Notre Dame Press, 1987).

——— 'Perfection and Creation' in Eleonore Stump (ed.), *Reasoned Faith* (Ithaca, NY and London: Cornell University Press, 1987).

Morriston, W., 'Is God Significantly Free?', *Faith and Philosophy*, 2 (1983), 257–63.

Parkinson, G. H. R., *Leibniz on Human Freedom* (Wiesbaden: Franz Steiner Verlag, 1970).

Plantinga, Alvin, *The Nature of Necessity* (Oxford: Oxford University Press, 1974).

Quinn, Philip L. 'God, Moral Perfection, and Possible Worlds', in Frederick Sontag and M. Darrol Bryant (eds.), *God: The Contemporary Discussion* (New York: The Rose of Sharon Press, Inc., 1982), 197–213.

Reichenbach, Bruce, 'Must God Create the Best Possible World?', *International Philosophical Quarterly*, 19 (1979), 208.

Reid, Thomas, *Essays on the Active Powers of Man*, vol. ii in *The Works of Thomas Reid, D.D.* (8th edn.), ed. Sir William Hamilton (Edinburgh, 1895).

Resnick, Lawrence, 'God and the Best Possible World', *American Philosophical Quarterly*, 10 (1973), 313–17.

Ross, Ian Simpson (ed.), 'Unpublished Letters of Thomas Reid to Lord Kames', *Texas Studies in Literature and Language*, 7 (1965), 51.

Rowe, W. L., 'Fatalism and Truth', *Southern Journal of Philosophy*, 18 (1980), 213–19.

——*Thomas Reid on Freedom and Morality* (Ithaca, NY and London: Cornell University Press, 1991).

——'The Problem of Divine Perfection and Freedom', in Eleonore Stump (ed.) *Reasoned Faith* (Ithaca, NY and London: Cornell University Press, 1993).

——'The Problem of No Best World', *Faith and Philosophy*, 11 (1994), 269–71.

——'Clarke and Leibniz on Divine Perfection and Freedom', *Enlightenment and Dissent*, 16 (1997), 60–82 (Special Issue on Samuel Clarke).

——'Can God Be Free?', *Faith and Philosophy*, 19 (2002), 405–24.

Swinburne, Richard, *The Christian God* (Oxford: Clarendon Press, 1994).

Talbott, Thomas, 'On the Divine Nature and the Nature of Divine Freedom', *Faith and Philosophy*, 5 (1988), 3–24.

Thomas, Mark L., 'Robert Adams and the Best Possible World', *Faith and Philosophy*, 13 (1996), 251–59.

Wainwright, William, 'Jonathan Edwards, William Rowe, and the Necessity of Creation' in Jeff Jordan and Daniel Howard-Snyder (eds.), *Faith, Freedom, and Rationality* (Boston: Rowman & Littlefield, 1996).

Wierenga, Edward, *The Nature of God* (Ithaca, NY: Cornell University Press, 1989).

——'The Freedom of God', *Faith and Philosophy*, 19 (2002), 425–36.

Yandell, Keith, 'Divine Necessity and Divine Goodness' in T. Morris (ed.), *Divine and Human Action* (Ithaca, NY and London: Cornell University Press, 1988).

Index

link b/t _necessity_ + non-gratefulness